Lecture Notes in Economics and Mathematical Systems 557

Salvatore Barbaro

Equity and Efficiency Considerations of Public Higher Education

Springer

Author

Salvatore Barbaro
Johannes-Gutenberg University
Department of Economics (FB03)
55099 Mainz, Germany
e-mail: barbaro@uni-mainz.de

Library of Congress Control Number: 2005928951

ISSN 0075-8442
ISBN-10 3-540-26197-4 Springer Berlin Heidelberg New York
ISBN-13 978-3-540-26197-1 Springer Berlin Heidelberg New York

Springer is a part of Springer Science+Business Media

springeronline.com

Printed in Germany

Typesetting: Camera ready by author
Cover design: *Erich Kirchner*, Heidelberg

Printed on acid-free paper 42/3130Di 5 4 3 2 1 0

To Yvonne

Christian Bruns, Carolin Dobler, Brian Frizelle, Marie Waller and Janina Pahmeier for excellent research assistance.

I am particularly indebted to Bob Haveman for the invitation to the La Follette School of Public Affairs at the University of Wisconsin-Madison, where Chapter 6 was written and reworked to a remarkable extent.

My good friend and witness to my marriage Daniel Schüle, who worked for different institutions in the field of higher education as a non-economist, often disregarded my ideas and conclusions for an alternative higher-education funding. His skepticism against model-based examinations helped me to see the political and social role of higher education through a different lens. I do not want to forget all of the disputes that I had with him.

I wish to express my gratitude with special emphasis to my good friend, former study mate and co-author, Jens Südekum. We discussed and developed our ideas, projects, and dreams for a just and better world for many years. I would not want to have missed this experience for anything.

In writing a thesis, one accumulates a long list of debts. I apologize to anyone who has been inadvertently left out of these acknowledgments.

Last, but certainly not least, I want to thank my beloved wife Yvonne. She made sure that no days were devoted solely to work on this thesis or any other project, even though much of the time for this project came at her expense. For her constant injection of wise perspective and exceptional companionship always, there are no adequate words. This book is dedicated to her with my heartfelt pledge: *You'll never walk alone!*

Mainz, May 2005 *Salvatore Barbaro*

Preface

The present book has been accepted as my PhD–thesis at the University of Göttingen on November 19, 2004. It was accomplished during the time period starting in January 2001, when I got the much-appreciated opportunity to work as a research assistant at the Institute of Public Economics.

I am particularly indebted to Prof. Dr. Helga Pollak, the former chair of the Institute of Public Economics, for her advice and the opportunity she gave me to work at the Institute. In March 2003, Professor Dr. Robert Schwager became her successor and also became my PhD advisor. I am grateful for his advice in many helpful discussions. I would also like to thank Professor Dr. Martin Kolmar from the Johannes-Gutenberg University, Mainz, who was the second member of my thesis committee. I benefit immensely from the fruitful and inspiring discussions with him.

I also want to thank Professor Dr. Walter Zucchini from the Institute of Statistics and Econometrics at the University of Göttingen. We shared many helpful conversations. In particular I had insightful discussion on the resampling methods used in the present work. Professor Zucchini was the third member of my thesis committee.

Some parts of this thesis were in circulation in several papers and were discussed by several people face-to-face and at international conferences. The three members of my thesis committee, Helga Pollak, Meta Brown (Madison/Wisc.), Elena Del Rey (Gironda), Andreas Haufler (Munich), Robert Haveman (Madison/Wisc.), Álvaro M. Pina (Lisabon), Panu Poutvaara (Copenhagen), Tara M. Sinclair (St. Lois), Jens Südekum (Konstanz), and Martin Teuber (Göttingen) were especially persistent in questioning my basic premises, challenging my conclusions, and forcing me to rethink and reformulate. The Deutsche Forschungsgemeinschaft, Universitätsbund Göttingen, Georg-August University of Göttingen, the German Central Bank, and the Johannes-Gutenberg University of Mainz provided financial support for attendance at very helpful conferences abroad. The HIS in Hannover helped me locate difficult–to–find data for the empirical part of this book. I also thank

Contents

1

Outline of the Book

It has become part of the conventional wisdom in the economics of education that subsidies to higher education have a regressive distributional effect. Given that relatively more children from wealthier families enroll in higher education, many economists assume that these subsidies to higher education have an unwanted distributional impact. *The nurse is being taxed to support the higher education of the dentist's son*, as it is sometimes bluntly put.

In Germany and possibly elsewhere, this reproach concerning fiscal activity in higher education is as old as the proposal to subsidize tuition fees. In 1875, the German Social Democratic Party (SPD) for the first time expressed in its *Gotha Program* the demand for "free instruction." Karl Marx and Friedrich Engels were the first to question this in their *Critique of the Gotha Program*: Free instruction "only means in fact defraying the cost of education of the upper classes from the general tax receipts" ((Marx and Engels, 1875[1962], p. 30); own translation).

Over a century later, the critique did not only come from the Marxists' side. The most popular economist who expressed the claim noted above was Milton Friedman. He asserted that public higher education produced a "perverse distribution of income" (Friedman, 1962, p. 105). For this reason, that thesis is henceforth referred to as the Friedman-thesis. The intuition of the Friedman-thesis is concerned with the processes of selection and allocation of students to the higher-education system. Given that children from upper-income families are more likely to obtain higher education than children from lower-income ones, it seems reasonable to assume that wealthier households gain the most from subsidies. In their book *Free to Choose* Milton and Rose Friedman express their opinion as follows:

> We know of no government program that seems to us so inequitable in its effects, so clear an example of Director's Law, as the financing of higher education. In this area those of us who are in the middle– and upper–income classes have conned the poor into subsidizing us on the grand scale—yet we not only have no decent shame, we boast

to the treetops of our selflessness and public–spiritedness. (Friedman and Friedman, 1979, p. 183)

In fact, many textbook writers still refer to this thesis, even though empirical work on this issue is at best inconclusive. Moreover, the literature often confuses a cross–sectional analysis and a long–run view. It is interesting to note that almost all empirical studies are cross-sectional analyses. As such an analysis provides a snapshot of distributional impact at particular points in time, the studies can be criticized for ignoring the longitudinal dimension of the point at issue. This critique also applies to the distributional effect of higher-education subsidies (see e.g. McGuire, 1976; Bowman et al., 1986; Pechman, 1972; Beckmann, 2003). In analyzing that effect, we have to distinguish between an analysis of children from various household types, and an analysis of educated and non-educated individuals throughout their lives. For the former, a cross–sectional examination is the only alternative; for the latter, the related literature uses a long-run analysis.[1]

The huge empirical literature on that issue, however, provides at most only scant evidence for this thesis. The debate started with the work of Pechman (1970), which contradicted the results provided by Hansen and Weisbrod (1969a). This disputation provoked a debate on the distributional effect that lasted nearly ten years, the "Hansen-Weisbrod-Pechman" debate (see Hansen and Weisbrod (1969a,b, 1971, 1978), Pechman (1970); Hartmann (1970); McGuire (1976); Conlisk (1977); Cohn et al. (1970)). Since then, a large number of studies are published. In Chapter 2 we present and review several examinations. Empirical evidence using GSOEP-data is provided in Chapter 3.

The literature covering the longitudinal approach is inconclusive. For example, building on Grüske (1994), García-Peñalosa and Wälde (2000) argue that "[i]f the average tax payer has a lower lifetime income than the average university graduate [. . .], a subsidy to higher education financed from general taxation implies reverse lifetime redistribution, i.e. redistribution from the poor to the rich." Although the paper provides several very enlightening results, this approach can be critically assessed with respect to two aspects. First, it does not distinguish sufficiently between the change of distribution between *rich* and *poor*, and that between graduates and non-graduates throughout their lives. Second, Pareto-improving subsidies can also be identified as *regressive* using this approach,[2] as shown in Sturn and Wohlfahrt (1999, 2000).

---

[1] See e.g. (Atkinson and Stiglitz, 1985, p. 263) who argue that "[i]n empirical work, the unit of analysis is typically taken as the nuclear family or household, and the distribution based on all such units in existence at a particular date. On the other hand, the lifetime approach seems more relevant to *individuals*. A person may belong to several different families during his life, and it makes little sense to regard him as changing identity on leaving or entering a nuclear family."

[2] In a subsection, García-Peñalosa and Wälde (2000) also ask whether a particular individual is better or worse off if education is subsidized. They point out that

However, the main question to which some papers address to is whether subsidies to higher education are granted at the expense of non-graduates. It is called *inequitable* if this question can be confirmed. Thus, we henceforth call subsidies *equitable* if also those not benefiting from such subsides directly because they do not attend higher education are better off.

A second strand is directly concerned with Pareto-superiority of subsidies to higher education. For example, Johnson (1984); Poutvaara and Kanniainen (2000); Dur and Teulings (2003, 2004) and Bovenberg and Jacobs (2005) argue that, at least in closed economies, subsidies to higher education may be to the mutual advantage of both graduates and non-graduates. Johnson (1984) argues that unskilled individuals may also prefer a tax–financed subsidy to higher education, because they reap part of the gains due to complementarities between skilled and unskilled labor. The specification of the production process of the economy is that aggregate output is a linear-homogenous function of three types of labor (high-skilled, medium-skilled, and low-skilled labor). This specification implies that complementarities (may) exist so that the low–skilled group may also benefit, although indirectly, from the subsidies. If this is the case, the higher-education subsidies are *equitable.*[3]

This viewpoint is interesting because it highlights a simultaneous effect of efficiency-enhancing subsidies on both, equity and efficiency. If human capital is seen as an *engine of economic growth*, or if subsidies to higher education raise the human-capital stock to an efficient level, or compensate for existing inefficiencies, it is possible that those who finance the subsidies through their taxes can demand compensation from those who benefit from the subsidies directly during their lifetime.[4] If such compensation is possible, the goals of efficiency and equity can be in harmony, i.e. subsidies to higher education are Pareto-superior. Otherwise, there is a trade-off.

Poutvaara and Kanniainen (2000) also deal with this argument. The main purpose of their paper is to study the possibility of a voluntary *social contract* benefiting all groups instead of a voting equilibrium where a minority is worse

---

it might be that all agents are better off after a subsidy has been introduced. Unfortunately, they do not compare the two approaches, nor do they demonstrate the circumstances under which this is possible. This is a gap that this thesis wishes to bridge.

[3] Johnson defines *equity* as follows: "The distribution of the burden of educational costs may be said to be equitable if both groups want the same size at the prevailing level of s. If the size is also efficient, this value of s is positive so long as low-skilled labor is not very much more complementary with medium than which high–skilled labor," where s denotes a certain fraction of the total social costs of the higher-education system.

[4] The basic intuition for that has been put forth very clearly by (Baran and Sweezy, 1966, p. 150): "If what government takes would otherwise not have been produced at all, it cannot be said to have been squeezed out of anybody. Government spending and taxing, which used to be primarily a mechanism for transferring income, have become, in large measure, a mechanism for creating income."

off. The distribution of the gains created by such a *social contract* depends on relative power, where the groups are engaged in Nash bargaining. However, free-rider behavior of the low-skilled agents in an open economy may undermine such a contract. Their willingness to commit to an educational subsidy vanishes as they anticipate the inflow of educated agents from abroad when the domestic rate of return on education exceeds that abroad.

Similar to Johnson (1984), Dur and Teulings (2003, 2004) develop a framework with skilled and unskilled workers as production inputs. The literature on the ability bias in the return to education indicates that education and innate ability are complementarities (see e.g. Angrist and Krueger, 1991). They emphasize that subsidies to all levels of education particularly favor those workers of high ability. Then, if such complementarities apply, optimism on the distributional effect may be discounted. Bovenberg and Jacobs (2005) regard distribution and subsidies to education as Siamese twins.

In this thesis, we emphasize the role of windfall gains that occur from subsidizing higher education. It is shown that the existence of windfall gains is likely to prevent subsidies from being Pareto-superior although they remain efficiency-enhancing. Non-graduates may be left worse off although aggregate net lifetime earnings—the sum of the net lifetime earnings of those who can and those who cannot attend higher education—are maximized when higher-education investments are subsidized up to an efficient level. This argument (i.e. that an equity-efficiency trade-off can occur due to windfall gains created by efficiency-enhancing subsidies) has been neglected in the literature so far.

The reason windfall gains occur if subsidies to higher education are organized as unconditional grants is the lack of information about agents' abilities. Nevertheless, it can be shown that a voluntary graduate tax (a similar proposal has been put forth recently by Poutvaara (2004)) can be regarded as a revelation mechanism so that alternative funding schemes are likely to break down the equity-efficiency trade-off. We show that such a voluntary graduate tax is a better means of achieving both efficiency and equity goals.

The necessary condition for Pareto-superior subsidies is the enhancement of efficiency. There would be no potential Pareto improvement by establishing public education in a first-best situation. As there are no imperfections, the laissez-faire outcome is Pareto-optimal.

In summary, the main argument of this literature is that the distributional effects are not necessarily inequitable (in the sense that they do not leave non-graduates worse off) because the agents can negotiate about the value-added. This argument, however, assumes that public higher education can be regarded as a means to enhance efficiency. We will, therefore, not confine ourselves to the distributional impact, but also consider some aspects of efficiency.

In the last decades, advocates of public activities in the education sector have particularly referred to externalities, credit constraints, and distributional issues.[5] The discussion about externalities gained more importance in the 1980s and 1990s, particularly because of the seminal paper of Haveman and Wolfe (1984) and because of new developments in growth theory, following the dismissal of earlier explanations based on neoclassical marginal productivity theory (cf. (Blaug, 1970, pp. 112ff)). However, the empirical evidence for positive externalities is scant at best (see Acemoglu and Angrist (2000); Bils and Klenow (2000); Krueger and Lindahl (2001) for recent contributions).

The importance of credit constraints is disputable as well. Capital-market imperfections, so the argument goes, may hinder poor agents financing the costs of obtaining higher education (see Saint-Paul and Verdier (1993); Perotti (1993); Benabou (2000, 2002)). However, there is little empirical evidence (see, e.g. Carneiro and Heckman, 2002; Cameron and Heckman, 2001; Keane and Wolpin, 2001). Friedman (1962) and others (see Epple and Romano (1998) for an overview) have persuasively argued that vouchers or student loans, for example, are a better means to compensate for unwanted effects that result from credit constraints. However, even if all classical arguments in favor of public subsidization cannot be dismissed as a whole, most economists argue that these arguments cannot justify the wide prevalence of education subsidies in many countries, in particular in Europe.

While earlier discussions were centered around the expenditure side of the budget, recent[6] contributions increasingly focus on revenue. The impact of taxes on human-capital accumulation has become the central element in the recent literature. Trostel (1993, 1996) has shown that taxation has a negative impact on human capital investments and that education subsidies should primarily be seen and justified as a compensation for this tax distortion. In making this argument, Trostel uses an econometric model with a proportional tax rate, and it is assumed that the direct costs of obtaining higher education are not tax-deductible.

Dupor et al. (1998) analyzed the distorting impact of progressive taxation based on US tax law in 1970. The findings show that progressivity led to an approximately 5-percent decline in human-capital investment in 1970. Based on data from 1990, the impact differed considerably depending on the choice of schooling, and lay between close to zero and −22%. Sturn and Wohlfahrt (2000) referred to the *foregone smoothing benefit*. Due to tax progression, combined with annual tax assessment, graduates pay more taxes than non-graduates with the same net lifetime earnings because graduates accumulate their income in a shorter period of time.[7] In summary, recent contributions

[5] See Barbaro (2003a) for a survey of empirical works on the issue.

[6] Previous examinations of the effect of taxation on human-capital accumulation are, e.g. Heckman (1976), and Eaton and Rosen (1980). In both works, labor-income taxation was found to have a neutral effect if the educational outcome is certain, but in both papers only the opportunity costs of obtaining higher education are considered.

[7] In addition, Wigger (2004) supported the implications of the above research in the case where subsidies to higher education are combined with optimal linear

have focused more on the inefficiencies created by taxation than on the positive externalities created by human-capital investment.

In these recent contributions and also in previous examinations (e.g. Heckman, 1976; Eaton and Rosen, 1980), investment in education is a continuous decision, i.e. homogenous agents optimize the time devoted to education. In practice, however, we observe that the investment decision in favor of higher education is made by some agents whereas others avoid higher education. In this thesis, we show that equity effects of education subsides differ remarkably if the educational-investment decision is *discrete*. The reason is that here the tax distortion affects only a fraction of the population instead of the whole, as in the aforementioned studies.

This thesis is organized as follows. Part I deals with the distributional implications which arise in the cross-sectional perspective. It presents an overview over several previous studies (Chapter 2). Then, a new empirical analysis for Germany is provided in Chapter 3. By doing so, we will deal with the problem of statistical inference which was often ignored in the previous literature and we will analyze the effect of a change in the net price for higher education where we will find a connection to the literature on the political economy of higher-education funding.

Part II deals with the long-run perspective. The starting point is an often cited examination done by Grüske (1994). We will critically assess the methodology and the results in Section 4.2 which concludes with our proposal for an adequate deal with the question concerning the distributional effect among graduates and non-graduates during their lifetime (Section 4.2.4).

In order to put forth our argument, we adopt the Model of Creedy and François (1990) which will be presented in Chapter 5. Built on this model, we will develop an amended framework in which our analysis takes place (Chapter 6). In that Chapter, we will first be concerned with the efficiency of subsidies to higher education in Section 6.3 and then address the distributional effects.

Against the background of this analysis we discuss various proposals for a higher-education funding reform (Chapter 7). In particular, we turn our attention to the concept of a graduate tax and to various kinds of student loans. In Section 7.1 however, a new scheme for higher-education funding is presented (and proposed): a voluntary graduate tax. It will be shown that this scheme is likely to achieve both aims, equity and efficiency, much better than the current practice in many European countries. Part III is related to efficient subsidies to higher education under progressive taxation. Chapter 10 summarizes and concludes with political implications. Part IV provides an appendix with further information and proofs.

---

income taxes à la Sheshinski (1972), but social welfare cannot be increased by supplementing a nonlinear income tax (in the tradition of Mirrless (1971)) with a subsidization of direct costs.

Summing up, the main objective of this thesis is to assess the widely-used tax-financed subsidy system and understand the impact of different degrees and kinds of subsidization on both efficiency and equity.

Part I

The Distributional Impact of Subsidies to Higher Education in the Cross-Sectional Perspective

2

Previous Studies

2.1 The Hansen-Weisbrod-Pechman Debate on the Distributional Effect of Education Subsidies in the US

The first empirical research on the distributional impact was carried out by Hansen and Weisbrod (1969a). In their article, they showed that worse-off households in California gain less from higher-education subsidies than better-off households even after allowing for the fact that they also contribute less in taxes to support public colleges and universities. Therefore, they reasoned that the Californian system of subsidizing higher education out of public funds redistributes income from the poor to the rich. Although they confirm a widespread thesis, they provoked a large debate on the distributional effect, called the "Hansen-Weisbrod-Pechman" debate, which lasted nearly ten years (see Hansen and Weisbrod (1969a,b, 1971, 1978), Pechman (1970); Hartmann (1970); McGuire (1976); Conlisk (1977); Cohn et al. (1970)).

Pechman was the first to oppose Hansen and Weisbrod's thesis. He argued, "At no point do Hansen and Weisbrod compare the benefits and costs of public higher education at different levels, as they seem to suggest. Their comparison is between benefits and taxes paid on the average by families with and without children enrolled in the California system." (Pechman, 1970, p. 361). Furthermore, he demonstrates that Hansen and Weisbrod's data can be reworked to turn their results upside down, so that the distributional effect becomes clearly progressive. A similar procedure, based on Hansen and Weisbrod's data (updated to 1971-72), was used by McGuire (1976). Additionally, he argued that the family group of which the head is between the ages of 35 and 60 years is the most appropriate universe with which to compare the income of student's parents, and that student financial aid must be added to tuition subsidies to obtain the total subsidy given to students in California public higher education. Taking into account these adjustments, McGuire concluded that the subsidy granted to students in each segment of public higher education in California was, both on the average and in the aggregate, larger for students from below-average-income families than for students from above-average-income families.

2.2 Several Studies for Various Countries: A Brief Review

Machlis (1973) for New York, Fields (1975) for Kenya, Crean (1975) for Canada, Merz (1981) for Switzerland, James and Benjamin (1987) for Japan and Lemelin (1992) for Quebec provided more empirical results. All of them used a net-transfer calculation. Except for Fields, Lemelin, and Merz, all authors found that the distributional impact is progressive. Merz concluded in favor of a proportional incidence, Fields determined the middle-income groups as the net gainers, and Lemelin found a regressive impact when parents' education is used to define the social position of families. Inadequate data might be the reason why none of these authors considered equivalence scales to define in a common way which households are wealthy and which are poor.

More recent studies use equivalence scales. Tsakloglou and Antoninis (1999) used equivalence-consumption expenditures for each household as an indicator for the household's welfare level. In order to judge to what degree inequality was reduced through public education on various levels, they used some inequality indices. Unfortunately, they did not consider the incidence of the tax burden to financing the subsidization, and they neglected some problems of statistical inference. These methodological problems aside, they hint at regressive effects for tertiary education. The first research using equivalence incomes and a net-transfer calculation was done by Sturn and Wohlfahrt (1999) for Austria in 1994. They concluded that public subsidization had a clearly progressive effect.

Regardless of the fact that empirical evidence is at least inconclusive, international research initiatives and textbooks often refer to the thesis of a regressive distributional impact, and many models take it for granted. Blaug (1982) was certainly right to ask in surprise: "How is it possible that so many commentators keep repeating the Hansen-Weisbrod results as if they were gospel truths?"

Next, we present and assess several previous studies on the distributional effect of public higher education in Germany. These studies are of special interest because we will provide new empirical evidence from Germany in Chapter 3.

2.3 Grüske's Cross-Section Study

The cross-sectional view in this and other similar papers is concerned with distributional impacts that are related to a particular year. In the following suggested approach, families should be classified by their gross household income per year. Both benefits in kind related to education, such as a tuition-free education, and all the other directly support benefits that students receive due to their status are considered.[1]

2.3.1 Method

All students are assigned to their household of origin. All households are divided into four income groups (*low, middle, elevated, high*) according to the social survey of the DSW from 1983. The contribution to the financing of public spending for higher education and the respective share on received payments are determined for each income group. In the end, it shall be possible to determine for each income group whether it is a net receiver or net contributor of the public financing of higher education.

2.3.2 Results

Grüske (1994) determines a distributional effect from households without students to those with students (Grüske, 1994, p. 103). Moreover, a distribution within households with students occurs from the two higher income groups to the two lower income classes. Thereby, those benefits that the two higher income groups do not receive have a special impact, e.g. benefits granted according to Bafög. The net results can be summed up as follows: for the income group *low* +3%[2], for *middle* +11%, for *elevated* +5% and, finally, for the income group *high* −19% (Grüske, 1994, p. 113f; Tables A6 and A7).

Grüske distinguishes between the absolute and relative net incidence, which describes the difference between received benefits and burden. For the lowest income bracket, the received benefits exceed the burden by more than fifty times (Grüske, 1994, p. 94). If the absolute net effects are applied to the gross incomes, the incidence is more balanced. "The lowest income bracket gains more than 30% of their income whereby the relative net effect for high incomes amounts to −9%" (Grüske, 1994, p. 94; own translation). "All in all, the politically desired preferential treatment of students from both, low-income households and non-employed families against other groups occurs" (Grüske, 1994, p. 101; own translation).

2.3.3 Discussion

Households are not weighted according to their size

Classifying households according to their unweighed incomes is problematic since a single person with an income of 2,500 currency units is treated as a

[1] These are, for example, benefits granted according to *student financial assistant scheme* (Bafög) and child benefits. Additionally, indirect benefits are considered with respect to the allowance time.

[2] 3% indicates that the portion of benefits this group receives is 3% above the portion they contribute in taxes

family with six members who have a household income of 2,500 units. The empirical literature therefore commonly generates adjusted incomes.[3]

The determination of teaching-related tax benefits is problematic

Moreover, it is not unproblematic to classify the granted tax benefits related to teaching. Due to the principle of non-affectation, there are no direct payments made to a particular budget for teaching-related university expenditures. Grüske has calculated that 60% of all university expenditures are spent for teaching. Therefore, 2% of a household's tax payments are defined as paid tax benefits for teaching-related university expenditures. Since this method of classification will be important for Grüske's long-run approach, it shall be discussed in further detail in Chapter 4.2.

The reference situation does not consider an adjustment reaction of individuals

The reference situation shall be defined as a condition in which no public financing of higher education takes place (in exchange to a tax cut). It is thereby assumed that alternative ways of financing higher education do not lead to adjustment reactions. This is certainly a very restrictive presupposition, as it is normally assumed that individuals react to price changes. Moreover, empirical investigations show that (in particular) lower income brackets react very elastically to price changes (cf. for instance, McPherson and Shapiro (1991), Shea (2000), Blossfeld and Shavit (1993), and Mare (1980, 1993)).

2.3.4 Summary

A methodical criticism of the examination design with respect to the cross-sectional view and the neglect of household sizes would probably lead to a slightly different final result. The trend, however, remains the same. Therefore, we can sum this up as follows: The distributional impacts in the cross section are progressive. A purely private financing of higher education would thus put a bigger strain on the lower income brackets due to their higher demand elasticity, hence leveling out the progressive distributional impact.

[3] The OECD provides both an older and a new equivalence scale, additionally, there is a social welfare assistance scale on basis of the *Social Security Code (Sozialgesetzbuch)* (which was reformed in 1990). Both the German Council of Economic Advisers (Sachverständigenrat zur Begutachtung der Gesamtwirtschaftlichen Entwicklung) and the German Institute of Economic Research (DIW) weight households with the square root of the number of their family members (Faik, 1998, p. 17).

2.4 Helberger's Testimonial for the Transfer-Enquête-Commission

In 1977, the German government established a committee of experts in order to determine the impact of public transfer incomes on the disposable income of private households. This so-called Transfer-Enquête-Commission finished its work in 1981 with the presentation of its final report. One of the testimonials which were requested by the commission was written by Christof Helberger who examined the "Impact of public spending on education in the Federal Republic of Germany on the income distribution of the education generation" (own translation). The primary data source was the income and consumption study ("Einkommens- und Verbrauchsstichprobe", EVS) of 1969.

2.4.1 Method and Results

By using a cross-section analysis, Helberger wanted to depict the relationship of the received spending on education to the net income of a household group as a group of origin of students. His survey led to the result that "[i]n 1969, the received spending on education for higher education and academic universities, in percent of net incomes of the respective group, rose with increasing income: Families with incomes between DM1500 and DM2000 per month[4] received university expenditures amounting to 0.7% of their net income, for families with an income of DM4000 to DM5000 , this percentage was 0.9%. The inequality of incomes was, thus, increased by the use of higher education" (Helberger, 1982, p. 55f) (own translation).

However, benefits granted as student aid, which have a strong progressive effect, were neglected due to the lack of data. Thus, the values determined for the lower income groups might have been strongly underestimated.

2.4.2 Discussion

Helberger determined values for ten income classes, but he only compared two of them in order to emphasize and justify his thesis of a regressive distributional impact. Regarding all ten values instead of only two, a negative correlation becomes evident which amounts to roughly −0.52. This can be explained by the fact that spending on education represents a relatively high share of income for the lower income groups. The value for the lowest income class comes to 3.79% and is, thus, almost 2.8 percentage points higher than the average. However, even if this group is removed from the data set, the other values still lead to a negative correlation of roughly −0.14.

Therefore, it can be concluded that only an arbitrary and not well justified selection of only two of ten values can support the thesis of a regressive distributional impact. The overall view disproves the theory and supports Grüske's

[4] DM denotes the former German currency *Deutsche Mark*.

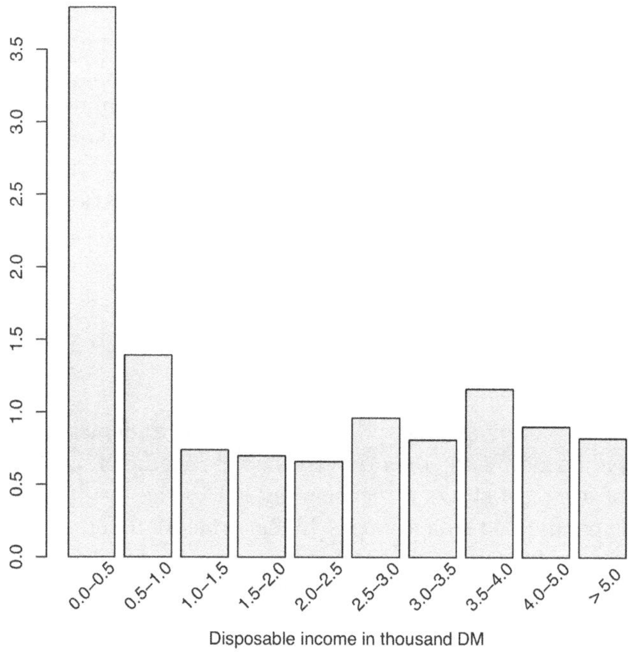

Fig. 2.1. Expenditure Incidence, reported by (Helberger, 1982, p. 30)

results, which were obtained in the cross-section for the distributional impact on families with students.

Moreover, the data basis is not unproblematic. Another reason for the high value of the lowest income group results from the fact that this class contains many student households as well. The EVS chooses households randomly in order to obtain data. Hence, it is not important whether pure student households or *classic* family households are chosen. If students live with their parents, they are assigned to their parents' household. If they live on their own, there is no such assignment. A student coming from a household with a net income of more than DM5,000 would, thus, be assigned to this household if she were living with her parents, but to a lower income class if she were leading her own household. Therefore, plenty of students are not assigned to their household of origin, which originally was a central concern of the study.

Another point of critique is the concentration on the expenditure incidence (incidence of public expenditure). It does become clear neither which tax amount the single household groups yielded nor which households are net gainers or net losers, respectively.[5] Probably due to a lack in the EVS data, only net incomes were applied. On the contrary, considering gross household incomes and formulating the incidence hypothesis would have made more sense: According to the incidence hypothesis, a proportional effect of the burden is assumed, regardless of the income size over all tax types (cf. (Grüske, 1994, p. 93)). Helberger points out that

> of each DM which accrues to the state via direct taxes, indirect taxes or other earnings of an income class, an amount at a value of the share of education expenditures on all revenues is being spent on the financing of education (Helberger, 1982, p. 54, (own translation)).

Combining both presuppositions, it could be assumed that each income group carries a tax burden for the universities in an equal relationship of their gross income. In that case, one could have set the received benefits in relation to the income, as was done by Helberger, whereas the benefits should be set in relationship to the gross, not the net income.

If Helberger had put the gross incomes at the basis, the values of Figure 2.1 would fall considerably with increasing income classes (i.e. with rising gross household incomes) since the progressivity of income taxation has to be considered. The correlation between household income on the one hand, and the ratio of received spending on education to the household income on the other hand, would in this case be even more negative. Thus, twisting Helberger's claim of a regressive distributional impact around completely.

Finally, it shall be mentioned that the households were also not weighted using equivalence scales.

2.5 Wrong Claim for Justice? A Tax-Incidence Approach

Krämer (1999) provides an interesting study which focuses on public revenues raised in order to finance higher-education subsidies. He emphasizes how much a particular income bracket contributes in taxes relative to the number of students it produces. This approach undoubtedly allows a better insight into the question about the *relative tax burden* of various income brackets. Nonetheless, some shortcomings should be emphasized that can be considered for further analyses using this approach.

Krämer has determined the taxes related to higher education that were paid by various income groups in a cross-section study. Moreover, he has calculated how many students S_i descend from each income group. Each income class i pays an amount αT_i to the universities. The tax amount per student

[5] Helberger justifies the concentration on the expenditure incidence with the argument that due to the principle of non-affectation the "distributional impact of revenues [...] are not directly a problem of financing education, but of the general tax and revenue policy" (Helberger, 1982, p. 55, (own translation)).

of income class i is denoted by $\frac{\alpha T_i}{S_i}$. Table 2.1 shows the values calculated for different income groups.

MDI_i	$\frac{\alpha T_i}{S_i}$
<2,000	12,000
2,000 – 3,000	9,100
3,000 – 4,000	9,300
4,000 – 5,000	11,000
>5,000	>12,000

Table 2.1. Monthly disposable income and tax contribution

MDI_i denotes the monthly disposable income of income group i. Krämer concludes from these values that, "this distribution from above to below which is caused by the so-called *free* higher education is a trivial consequence of the fact that families with low incomes rarely send their children to a university. They pay less in taxes, but compared to the return these contributions are still too high. Per child which they send to a university, the poor pay more than the rich." (Krämer, 1999, p. 402)(own translation).

Unfortunately, Krämer does not indicate how much the income class with the highest net income per month contributes exactly. It is only stated that the contribution exceeds DM12,000. Apparently, unweighed household incomes are of concern since the author does not refer to a conversion to equivalence numbers. In any case, the data point to a positive correlation, if one neglects the lowest income group.

It is worth a closer look at the lowest income group since it is apparently concerned with households of singles. Those households either do not include students or the student itself represents a household. Only a small part of households who belong to this income bracket with a net income of less than DM2,000, should be households with several members (i.e. families).

Insofar as the group of non-student single households was included in this class, the share of students in this group is low and, therefore, the costs per student are high. If, additionally, those single households are included which only consist of a student, these households are in any case net gainers (since students normally receive larger benefits from studying than they pay taxes). At this point, the weakness of Krämer's approach (to include only the costs) becomes particularly obvious.

Due to these methodological problems, it would be appropriate to exclude this group. However, even if the lowest income class were not excluded, the figures would not point to a regressive distributional impact. Instead there would be a distributional impact pointing to the middle incomes. It is only those values that would fall below the average.

In contrast to Helberger, who regards only the received benefits explicitly, Krämer solely includes the contributions of each income group. Thereby, received benefits (especially the educational advancement) have clearly progressive distributional impacts.

2.6 Summary and Comparison of the Cross-Section Studies

The studies that we have looked at above, provide four different methods with which to determine the distributional impacts. Let Ξ denotes a parameter which is relevant for the respective income group. It can be ascertained according to Grüske by:

$$\Xi_{G1} \equiv \phi_i L - \alpha T_i$$

if the absolute net incidence is concerned and, ibid., by

$$\Xi_{G2} \equiv \frac{\phi_i L - \alpha T_i}{Y_i^b}$$

if the relative net incidence is concerned. According to Helberger it is given by

$$\Xi_H \equiv \frac{\phi_i L}{Y_i}$$

and according to Krämer by

$$\Xi_K \equiv \frac{\alpha T_i}{S_i}.$$

The received portion of the entire benefits from higher education (L) is denoted by ϕ with $\sum_{i=1}^{n} \phi_i = 1$. The value ϕ_i positively correlates to the number of students from group i. α represents the share of tax payments which are ascribed to the universities, Y represents the net income (the superscript b denotes the gross income), S the number of students, and T denotes the total amount of taxes. The index i labels the respective income class. Since the cross-section analysis is concerned with distributional impacts within the same period, a time index is neglected.

Krämer does not consider the received benefits, but only the relative tax contribution. However, specific transfers, such as the Bafög (the German student financial assistance scheme), have an inevitably progressive effect. Krämer criticizes that "the story of an equitable free higher education cannot be wiped" out, irrespective of [the existence of] several respectable studies" (Krämer, 1999, p. 402) (own translation). Astonishingly, Grüske's study is one of these studies that Krämer refers to, whereas Krämer contradicts Grüske's cross-section results.

It is likely that the failure to consider equivalence incomes has the effect that all studies underestimate the progressive distributional impact. The reference situation, which all studies apply, is difficult to figure out. None of the contributions state how the distribution would have developed without the public financing of higher education. All authors assign a crucial role of the number of students from one income group. However, it would have had to be discussed if a pure private financing of higher education would lead to the effect that the number of students from the lowest income class fell more sharply than the number of students from higher income groups.

By indexing the relevant parameter Ξ according to Krämer's approach by taking the logarithm and differentiating it with respect to time, we get $w_{\Xi_K} = w_\alpha + w_{T_i} - w_{S_i}$. If the privatization of the costs of higher education results in the fall of the income tax rates (*differential incidence*), while this privatization at the same time lowered the number of students from an income group, it would be decisive whether $w_{T_i} - w_{S_i}$ is larger, smaller, or equal to 0. The same applies to Grüske's relative net incidence and to Helberger.

3

Empirical Evidence Using GSOEP Data

3.1 Methodology and Data

Even if the *Hansen-Weisbrod-Pechman debate* does not provide a final result for the distributional impact, it is generally agreed, with regard to methodology, that a net-transfer calculation is appropriate (cf. Blaug (1982)). The idea of such a calculation is to break down the population of households into income groups and then to check whether each income group gains more or less in subsidy benefits than it pays in taxes in order to support higher education. The pattern of such net-transfers depends on (*a*) the distribution of the benefits from public higher education along with (*b*) the tax-incidence effect. The tax incidence, resulting from both, the comprehensive tax rate structure and the distribution of the tax base among income brackets, will determine the implicit share of the costs of higher-education subsidies being imposed on each income class. The distribution of the benefits depends particularly on the student-representation effect, that is, whether each income bracket contributes a *pro-rata* share of students to the higher-education system. Furthermore, but to a lesser extent, the distribution of the benefits depends on their structure, which is the incidence of the benefits within households with children enrolled in higher education.

If the benefits attributable to a particular income bracket, as determined by the share of students it contributes, differ from its implied share of the cost of subsidization, as determined by the tax incidence among income brackets, then a transfer among these income brackets has occurred.

It is interesting to note that almost all studies use a net-transfer calculation. The main advantage of this method is obviously its clarity. It is less difficult to explain the results from a net-transfer calculation to policymakers than to explain them a regression analysis,[1] what economists often use. The reason why we also use the net-transfer calculation is indeed the fact that

[1] With, for instance, some socio-economic variables as exogenous elements and the difference between received benefits and contributed taxes as endogenous variable.

it is the standard method to analyze this point. On the other hand, such a calculation is involved with serious problems concerning statistical inference. A main advantage of regression analysis is its (automatic) implementation of an inference check. A main disadvantage of many alternative methods is the missing attempt to statistical inference.

Hence, the main goal of the present empirical examination is twofold. First, it provides new evidence on a persistent controversy. Second, it proposes a procedure to consider the need for statistical accuracy. By doing so, the bootstrap is proposed as an advisable method for computing confidence intervals. More details on bootstrapping are provided in Subsection 3.1.5.

3.1.1 Tax Incidence

How much an income bracket contributes to finance higher-education subsidies depends on the tax system. By paying taxes, all households carry the costs of subsidization. If $X\%$ of the public budget is spent for subsidies, every household will therefore provide $X\%$ of his tax burden for (this) fiscal activity. Since the comprehensive tax burden should be considered (direct as well as indirect taxes) and there is no detailed data concerning the tax incidence, the assumption of a proportional tax incidence shall be made. This assumption implies that the regressivity of indirect taxation offsets the progressivity of direct taxation. Empirical work for both, the German and the U.S. case (Grüske (1978), Pechman (1986)) indicates that this assumption is an acceptable approximation of the incidence of the tax burden[2] and it is also used in the studies by Sturn and Wohlfahrt (1999) and Grüske (1994). As a consequence, each income bracket contributes a portion of the whole tax revenues that is exactly the portion of gross income that each income bracket receives.

3.1.2 The Distribution of the Benefits

The amount of benefits a population subgroup receives depends in particular on the student-representation effect and on the structure of the benefits, as noted above. In Germany, households with students receive in-kind benefits from the higher-education system (tuition-fee subsidy). Additionally, they are granted a child benefit or child allowances (the latter only if its relief exceeds their child benefit). If a household does not gain from income-splitting (e.g. due to a divorce), it has the opportunity to demand an allowance called *Haushaltsfreibetrag*. Furthermore, every household with children enrolled in the education system can ask for an education allowance (*Ausbildungsfreibetrag*) as well as for other benefits in tax laws, which are not considered in the present study.[3]

[2] For a further discussion see (Haveman, 1988, Ch. 5).

[3] In 1997, an amount of DM220 per month (Child benefit) was granted for the first and second child, DM300 for the third and DM350 for the fourth, fifth and

Students and/or households also receive cash benefits through the student financial assistance scheme (Bafög). Since a large share of public higher-education funding consists of research and health expenditures, the amount of in-kind benefits every student/household receives cannot be measured exactly. According to a procedure developed by the Federal Statistical Office of Germany, the share of pure health expenditure on the entire expenditures for medical university institutions are estimated by the formula $\frac{AR}{CE-ES}$, where AR denotes the administrative revenues, CE denotes the current expenditure and ES denotes the revenues from external sources.[4]

Using this procedure, $\frac{AR}{CE-ES}$ amounts to 75.6%. Furthermore, we allocate half of the rest (distributed to non-medical faculties) as public subsidization, according to a procedure proposed by the Wissenschaftsrat[5] (cf. (Wissenschaftsrat, 1997, p. 32f)). Thus, every household with a student receives an amount of DM532 per month as in-kind benefit from public funding of higher education.

Apart from the in-kind benefits and the student financial assistance scheme, the remaining cash benefits are part of the general family promotion program and not part of the higher-education subsidies in the narrower sense. But the entitlement of these cash benefits would expire if the children were not enrolled in higher education. Therefore, it seems indispensable to take these benefits and the tax burden into consideration, in that taxes are necessary to finance these kinds of indirect higher-education subsidies.

The extent to which students receive cash benefits from Bafög depends primarily on the income of their parents. The basic intention of the Bafög is to enable children from low-income households to obtain higher education and is only granted to this group. Therefore, the incidence of Bafög is unambiguously progressive. On the other hand, it is obvious that the relief due to the various allowances (measured in absolute quantities) increases in income as a result of income-tax progression. The incidence of such an allowance is less clear-cut on measuring the relief in relative terms.

The incidence of the tax burden is henceforth referred to as *revenue incidence* (taxes being revenue of the state) and the incidence of the benefits is henceforth referred to as *expenditure incidence*. The difference is the result of the net-transfer calculation and can be called the *net incidence* (cf. Grüske (1994)).

---

so forth. Better-off households received a child allowance of DM288 (divorced parents) and DM576 (married parents). The *Haushaltsfreibetrag* was a monthly allowance of DM468, and the *Ausbildungsfreibetrag* was DM200.

[4] The author is grateful to Heinz-Werner Hetmeier from the Federal Statistical Office, Wiesbaden for helpful advice concerning that issue and to an anonymous referee of the *Finanzarchiv* for a helpful remark.

[5] The Wissenschaftsrat is an advisory body to the Federal Government and the state (Länder) governments. Its function is to draw up recommendations on the development of higher-education institutions, science, and the research sector with respect to content and structure, as well as on the construction of new universities.

If there are no subsidies, the net transfer for all income groups will be equal to zero. Therefore, the situation without public higher-education funding is the one to which the observed situation will be compared. If an arbitrary income bracket obtains a positive net transfer, it will gain from public subsidization, and vice versa.

3.1.3 Income Brackets

As noted above, the population of households will be broken down into income brackets, namely income deciles based on equivalized disposable income. The equivalence elasticity is simply set to one half. This so-called square-root scale is an application of the single parametric approximation to equivalence scales which encompassed a wide range of scales in use, first proposed by Buhmann et al. (1988).

3.1.4 Data

The data is taken from the 15th social survey (bmbf (1999b)). In this survey, the monthly net-incomes of students' parents have been listed. Additionally, the students specified the number of brothers and sisters living in the household of their parents and whether or not their parents were living together in the same household. Using these numbers, the household size is taken into account using the just-introduced equivalence scales, to obtain a weighted distribution of net-income. The sample contains $11,509$ households. See Appendix C for further details. Data for the income distribution of the whole population is taken from the German Socio-Economic Panel (GSOEP, see, for further details, Appendix A). Some summarizing statistics are provided in Appendix D.

3.1.5 Statistical Inference

A major shortcoming of the literature about income inequality is the lack of statistical inference ; in most studies, no attempt has been made to determine the statistical significance of observed differences in the computed values of a particular measure. As Mills and Zandvakili (1997) pointed out, the need for statistical inference with small samples should be obvious, but even for large samples, it may be essential to report statistical measures of precision. Since confidence-interval estimates available from asymptotic theory may not be accurate (see for further details Mills and Zandvakili (1997) and Biewen (2002)), an advisable method for computing confidence intervals is to bootstrap. These intervals so obtained have been shown to be superior to asymptotic intervals, both theoretically and in a variety of applications.[6]

[6] E.g. Burr (1994) studied bootstrap confidence intervals for three types of parameters in Cox's proportional hazards model, Mills and Zandvakili (1997) using the

In this chapter, bias-corrected and accelerated confidence intervals (BC_a) are computed. The BC_a-method is an improved version of the percentile method and is second-order correct in a wide class of problems.

Let $\hat{\theta}$ be an estimator of a parameter z. The percentile interval $(\hat{\theta}_{lb}, \hat{\theta}_{ub})$ of intended coverage 1-2α, is obtained directly from these percentiles. Therefore, $(\hat{\theta}_{lb}, \hat{\theta}_{ub}) = (\hat{\theta}^{*(\alpha)}, \hat{\theta}^{*(1-\alpha)})$, where $\hat{\theta}^{*(\alpha)}$ indicates the $100 \cdot \alpha^{th}$ percentile of B bootstrap replications. Percentiles of the bootstrap distribution also give the BC$_a$ intervals endpoints, but they further depend on an accelerator (acc) and the bias-correction (z_0). The BC$_a$ interval of intended coverage $1 - 2\alpha$, is given by $(\hat{\theta}_{lb}, \hat{\theta}_{ub}) = (\hat{\theta}^{*(\alpha_1)}, \hat{\theta}^{*(\alpha_2)})$, where

$$\alpha_1 = \Phi\left(\hat{z}_0 + \frac{\hat{z}_0 + z^{(\alpha)}}{1 - acc(\hat{z}_0 + z^{(\alpha)})}\right),$$
$$\alpha_2 = \Phi\left(\hat{z}_0 + \frac{\hat{z}_0 + z^{(1-\alpha)}}{1 - acc(\hat{z}_0 + z^{(1-\alpha)})}\right).$$

Here $\Phi(\cdot)$ is the standard normal cumulative distribution function and $z^{(\alpha)}$ is the $100\alpha^{th}$ percentile point of a standard normal distribution (for further details see Efron and Tibshirani (1993)).

3.2 The Distribution of Children from Various Income Brackets in the German Higher-Education System

As noted above, the distribution of the benefits among the income deciles depends particularly on the number of children each income decile sends to the higher-education system. Figure 3.1 depicts the distribution of children from various income brackets enrolled in higher education compared with the entire population. The horizontal line indicates the entire population. Every income decile consists of 10% of the whole population, in view of the definition of income deciles. The filled bars indicate whether households with children enrolled in higher education are over- or under-represented. The lines around the bars indicate the confidence intervals with 95% confidence.

For example, 10% of the entire population is part of the bottom decile, but only roughly 7.65% of all students are descended from it, and hence the bottom decile is significantly under-represented in higher education. The same applies to the second and the third decile but also to the top one. The fourth and fifth deciles are neither under- nor over-represented in higher education (because the confidence intervals overlap the 10%-line), but there is over-representation of the sixth to the ninth deciles. It is important to note that

bootstrap percentile method proposed by Efron and Tibshirani (1993); Xu (2000) appealing inference using the iterated-bootstrap method proposed by Hall (1992). See also Mac Kinnon (2002) for a recent survey on the role of bootstrap inference in econometrics.

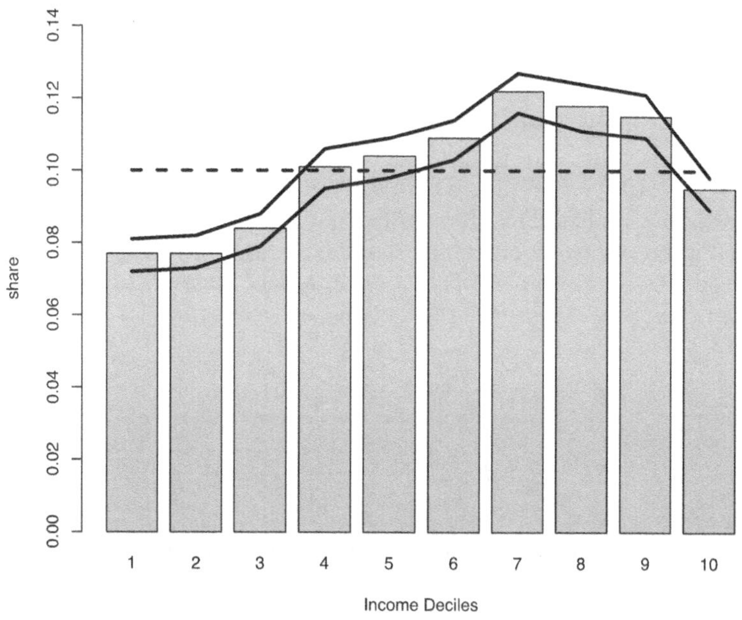

Fig. 3.1. The Distribution of Children from various income brackets enrolled in higher education compared with the entire population. Source: bmbf, GSOEP, own calculations

though an unevenness in the distribution can be discerned, only a slight under-representation of the bottom and of the top decile and only a slight over-representation of the upper deciles can be observed. Thus, it seems to be true that better-off households enroll more children in higher education, but this over-representation is not excessive.

3.3 Net-Transfer Calculation

3.3.1 The Distribution of the Benefits (Expenditure Incidence)

The filled bars in Figure 3.2 show the distribution of benefits among the income deciles. It can be seen that the benefits are more or less evenly distributed, regardless of the fact that the students are unevenly distributed.

The bottom to the third deciles receive disproportionately large shares of all the benefits (e.g. roughly 7.65% of the students are enrolled from the bottom decile, but the same decile receives 11.31% of the benefits), which is primarily attributed to the student financial assistance scheme. The contrary applies to the other deciles. They receive a portion of the whole benefits that is below the share of the enrolled students. Only a small share of these subgroups benefits from Bafög, and the relief due to allowances is small in comparison to

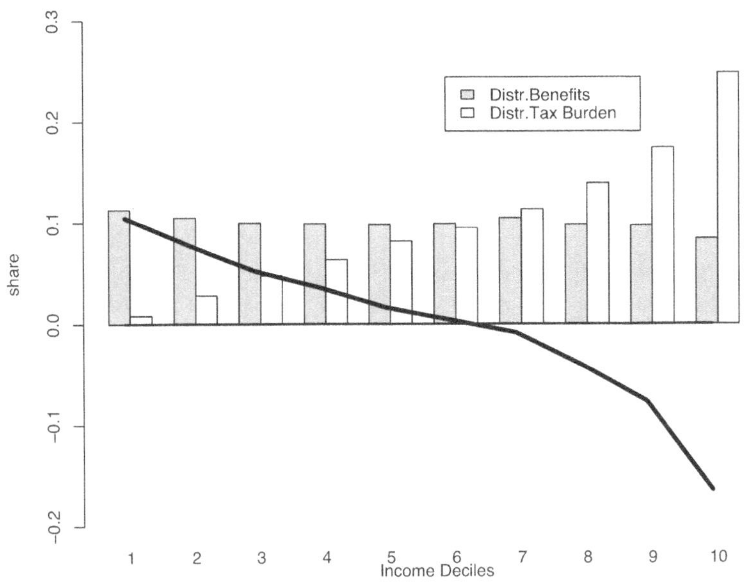

Fig. 3.2. Net Incidence. Source: bmbf, GSOEP, own calculations

the upper deciles. The relationship between received benefits and enrollment is only slightly disproportionate for the two uppermost deciles. They also do not profit from Bafög but they receive relief from the allowances that is relative high, caused by income tax progression.

3.3.2 The Distribution of the Tax Burden (Revenue Incidence)

The unfilled bars in Figure 3.2 show the tax incidence. According to the assumption made in regard to the comprehensive tax rate structure, the distribution of the tax burden is the same as the distribution of the gross income. Since the top decile receives (roughly) 24.86% of the whole gross income, the households in it also contribute 24.86% of the fiscal revenue and, therefore they provide about a quarter of the whole revenue to support higher-education subsidies.

3.3.3 Net Incidence

Figure 3.2 also shows the net incidence for each income decile. The bottom decile receives 11.3% of all the benefits, but contributes only 0.8% of the taxes to support it. By subtracting the tax burden from the received benefit portion, we see that the bottom decile gains, with a net transfer of approximately 10.5%. The lowest five deciles receive a significantly positive net transfer and the seventh to the top deciles a negative one. In the absence of public benefits, each income decile would pay exactly for what it receives, and therefore no income bracket could gain from redistribution through fiscal activity in higher education. To sum up, the analysis indicates that the distributional impact is clearly progressive.

3.4 Interpretation

How can these findings be explained? The intuition of Friedman and others is based on the processes of selection and allocation of students (unequal opportunities), as mentioned before. The probability that a child from a poor household will be enrolled in higher education is lower than the probability for a child from a rich household. At no point do we contradict this commonly observed fact (cf. Shea (2000); Blossfeld and Shavit (1993); McPherson and Shapiro (1991); Mare (1980)), but acknowledging this point alone does not suffice to establish a distributional effect. The problem of unequal opportunities is arguably a structural effect, and it may be over-compensated by a level effect, which is the general social stratification among and within the income deciles. Figure 3.3 shows the distribution of households with and without children within the income deciles (also for 1997). According to our cross-sectional view, only children who are actually part of their parents' household are taken into account. The top decile consists of 83% of households without children (DINKs, single households and elder married couples), and the proportion of households with children in the fifth decile is about 2.5 times as large as that in the top decile. The consequence of this result is that the probability of enrolling a child in higher education has to be about 2.5 times larger for members of the top decile compared to members of the fifth one in order to enroll the same number of students. This is the consequence of the level effect.

Roughly speaking, there are not enough children in top-decile households who could get a higher education even if children from such households were enrolled with relatively high probability. Children are concentrated in the intermediate deciles, whereas DINK households constitute the majority in the upper deciles (53% of all households at the top decile are DINK-households). The under-representation of the bottom deciles could also be explained by social stratification: pensioners and young single-parent households constitute the majority of the bottom decile. None of these households could *produce* students, at least in the cross-sectional view.

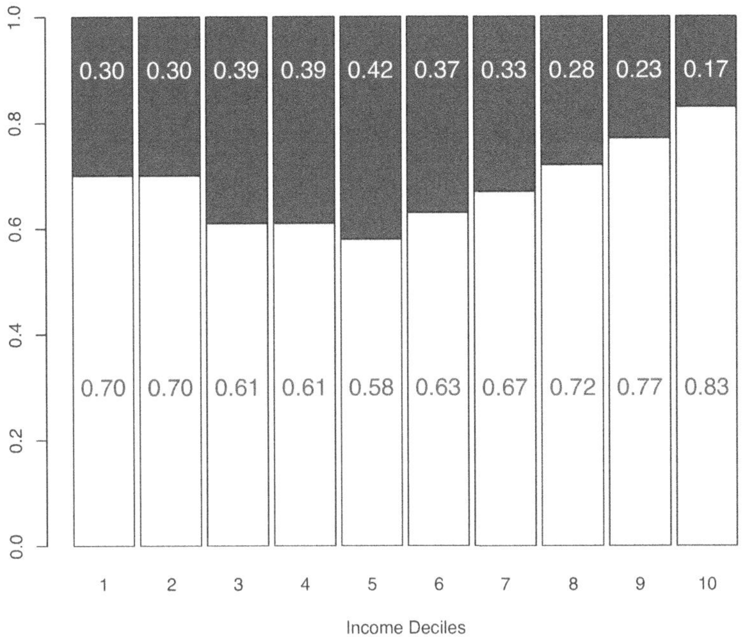

Fig. 3.3. The distribution of households with and without children among the income deciles. The filled bars indicate the households with children. Source: own calculations based on GSOEP data.

3.5 Extensions

3.5.1 A Change of the Net Price and its Effect on the Net Incidence

Analyzing the distributional effect of a modified net price of obtaining higher education (i.e. through an abolition of the student aid or of a reduction of the tuition fee subsidy) is another interesting issue with respect to policy implications. We could not simply rework the net transfer curve from Figure 3.2 by subtracting the benefits from the student aid, because a correlation between the grant of this cash benefit and the enrollment behavior seems likely. McPherson and Shapiro (1991) investigated the overall relationship between student aid and enrollment. Their analysis demonstrates that changes in the net price (e.g. a decrease in student aid) in the case of lower-income students has significant effects on their enrollment behavior. On the other hand, the elasticity of students from better-off households is supposed to be (very) small. Assume that all students from the bottom decile would not be enrolled if a repeal of the student aid occurred. In that case, the lower deciles would have a negative net transfer effect, because they would contribute by means of taxes in order to provide for the remaining benefits, but would not gain from any of

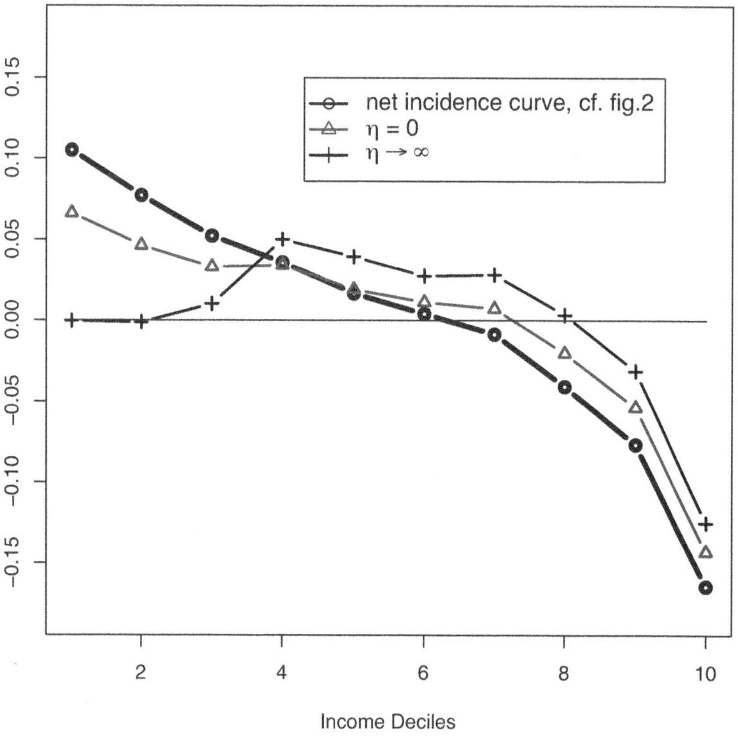

Fig. 3.4. Alternative scenarios for a repeal of the student aid with various elasticities of demand. η indicates the elasticity of enrollment with respect to the student aid. Source: own calculations

them. In other words: the isolated effect of a benefit can only be investigated precisely if we consider the enrollment elasticity with respect to the net price. Unfortunately, there is no data available about these elasticities for the various income brackets.

To achieve at least an approximation of the distributional impact caused by an abolition of the student aid, two scenarios are constructed. An elasticity equal to zero is assumed in the first scenario; thus, no student would change his or her enrollment behavior facing a change in the net price. In the second scenario, an infinitely large elasticity is assumed. In this case, the enrollment behavior changes considerably.

The bold line (indicated by circles) in Figure 3.4 is taken from Figure 3.2. The line indicated by triangles shows the net incidence resulting from the first scenario (elasticity $\eta = 0$) and the third line (indicated by crosses) shows the net incidence resulting from the assumption of $\eta \to \infty$. It is obvious that the second case leads to a situation in which the lowest deciles become net-payers and the changes in the net price clearly favor the intermediate deciles. Furthermore, even when enrollment behavior remains unchanged (as in the former scenario), an abolition of the Bafög scheme is shown to cause substantive regressive effects.

This result is congruent with predictions from the political-economy literature. In their paper, Fernandez and Rogerson (1995) show in a political-economy model that transfers of resources from lower income brackets to higher ones are possible if households vote over the extent to which they subsidize education. If education is only partially subsidized, poorer households that are credit-constrained cannot afford to obtain higher education and are thereby excluded from benefiting from the subsidies.

3.5.2 The Effect of the Equivalence Elasticity

As noted above, the equivalence elasticity is set to $\frac{1}{2}$ so as to compute roughly equated income deciles. Recent studies use the so-called modified OECD scale. The modified OECD scale assigns a normalized weight of unity to the household head, a weight of 0.5 to each remaining adult (including children older than 15 years) and a weight of 0.3 to each younger member of the household. The two equivalence scales produce similar results for most of the unweighted samples (e.g. a family with two adults and two young children is weighted with the factor $2.1 (= 1 + 0.5 + 0.3 + 0.3)$ using the modified OECD scale and weighted with the equivalence digit $2.0 \, (= \sqrt{4})$ using the square-root scale). But the equivalence factors differ significantly if children are aged over 15 years, which applies to enrolled students, because in contrast to the modified OECD scale the square-root scale does not take into account decreasing economies of scales with increasing age of children.

Figure 3.5 compares the alternative use of the equivalence scales. It follows from these differences in the equivalence factors that, by comparing the entire population with the subgroup of households having children enrolled in higher education, the alternative use of the modified OECD scale yields different results. Therefore, the portion of households with children enrolled in higher education will be higher in the lower deciles if one uses the modified OECD scale. While the net-transfer calculation depends in particular on the student-representation effect, the use of the square-root scale is more conservative (i.e. yields a less progressive distributional impact). Previous studies from the 1970s did often not take into account household size. The unweighted income level of a household was treated as a proxy for its level of welfare, with the argument that, at the very least, income is the means to achieve welfare. It has become part of the conventional methodology to use equivalized incomes. One can expect that their use affects the findings, as equivalizing makes the households with children look poorer. It could be presumed that some households that are part of an intermediate decile would be part of an upper one if unequivalized income levels were used, and vice versa. It is interesting to note that, on performing the same procedure as in the previous sections, the picture does not change strongly. Most households remain in

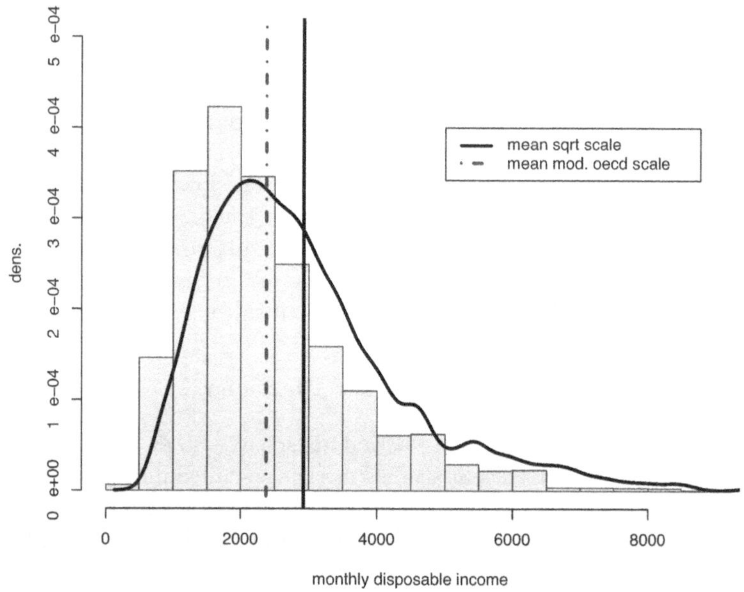

Fig. 3.5. Net income distribution of households with children enrolled in higher education—equivalence scales compared. Source: bmbf, own calculations.

their original decile or take a step upwards or downwards. The correlation coefficient is about 0.83.

3.5.3 The Distributional Impact Within Households with Children Enrolled in Higher Education

The effect of public subsidization on the income distribution is twofold. First, it affects the distribution among all households in the population and, second, it affects the income distribution within the population subgroup of the net gainers, that is, the households with children enrolled in higher education. Since the package of benefits consists of in-kind benefits (tuition fee subsidy), direct cash benefits, and indirect benefits through allowances, the distributional impact of these allowances is not clear-cut, due to income tax progression. Using Theil's entropy measure[7]

$$T(Y) = \frac{1}{n} \sum_i \left(\frac{Y_i}{\bar{Y}} \right) \cdot \log \left(\frac{Y_i}{\bar{Y}} \right)$$

[7] We use Theil's entropy measure because it is suitable for decomposition analysis. The better-known Gini coefficient "cannot be decomposed neatly into the *within* and *between* group term required by additive decomposability, which may lessen its appeal in certain applications." (Sen, 1997, p. 153f).

(where $\bar{Y}$ indicates the mean of the incomes over all individuals i, and n indicates the number of observations, respectively), we might ask:

1. Does public subsidization lead to a significant change in the income distribution and,
2. if it does, which benefits affect to which extent the final change?

Result 1
T falls from 0.1233 (before subsidization) to 0.0708 (after subsidization) and the confidence interval of the difference[8] (99 % confidence) does not overlap 0 (+0.0481 , +0.0572). Therefore, this result is significant.

In order to answer the second question, we use the decomposition rule for T, as expressed in Shorrocks (1982):

$$s_k = \frac{S_k}{T(Y)} = \frac{\Sigma_i Y_{ik} \cdot \log\left(\frac{Y_i}{\bar{Y}}\right)}{\Sigma_i Y_i \cdot \log\left(\frac{Y_i}{\bar{Y}}\right)}$$

where S_k might be regarded as the contribution of factor k to overall income inequality, and s_k indicates the proportional factor contributions. $\bar{Y}$ indicates the mean.

Result 2

Disposable income without subsidization	1.1773	(1.1619; 1.1842)
Child Benefit / Child allowances	-.0179	(-.0183 ; -.0174)
Other Allowances	-.0072	(-.0074 ; -.0072)
Bafög	-.0904	(-.0957 ; -.0861)
In-Kind	-.0634	(-.0634 ; -.0608)

(Bootstrap BC_a-confidence intervals with 99% confidence in brackets, 1000 replications)

A single benefit reduces inequality if its s_k is negative in sign. It reduces inequality significantly, if the confidence intervals do not overlap zero. It can be shown that each benefit reduces T significantly, but there is only a negligible effect of the allowances.

3.5.4 A Differential Incidence Approach

Hitherto, we have considered a condition in which no public financing of higher education takes place as the reference situation. Public subsidization, once established, requires higher taxes and the net-transfer calculation measures the incidence of both, the subsidies and the additional taxes levied in order to finance these subsidies. This concept of incidence has customarily been used in the related literature. Nevertheless, one might argue that other reference

[8] The procedure here is analogous to the comparison of two means from two different samples as it is for example well-known from a simple t-test. Consider the statistic $D = I_1 - I_2$, where I_1 and I_2 are two values of the Theil measure. The distribution of D can be bootstrapped in the same way used to obtain distributions of the two values I_1 and I_2.

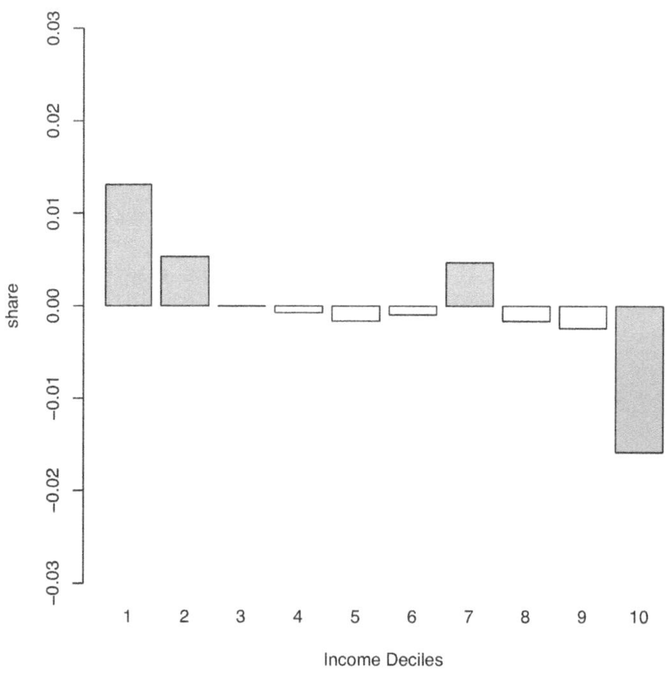

Fig. 3.6. Results of a differential-incidence approach. Source: see Figure 3.2.

situations are also suitable. For instance, consider the case where public expenditures and revenue are held constant. In this case, one expenditure scheme is substituted for another while taxes are held on the same level. The only change we consider is that the taxes levied in order to finance the higher-education promotion are alternatively spent for a lump-sum transfer which is uniformly distributed among all households. An income decile, then, is net-gainer of a higher-education subsidy if it receives more than 10% of the benefits from subsidization and vice versa.

The bars in Figure 3.6 show the difference between the 10% of the entire lump-sum transfer which each income decile would receive in the alternative scenario and the expenditure incidence which has been derived in Figure 3.2. As can be seen, the differences are very small. The main result is that no gainer or looser can be ascertained. The gray bars indicate that the difference to zero is not significantly different on a 95% level and the white bars indicates that the difference is not significant on a 90% level.

Hence, by considering this approach, the distributional effect of public higher education is neither progressive nor regressive, but neutral. This approach, however, unveils that it can be important to ask whence the resources are squeezed out. As an example, if public subsidization is financed in exchange for a social-security cut, the result obtained so far might turn upside down.

3.6 Conclusion

In the last decades, discussing the consequences of a given unwanted distributional impact of public higher education has become more and more important. Only to a lesser extent has there been focus on empirical investigations, the need for which has been ignored by both textbook authors and model constructors.

So far, no one had analyzed the distributional impact by using a net-transfer calculation with equivalized income data and with notes on statistical inference. Only Sturn and Wohlfahrt (1999) considered the net-transfer calculation and used weighted-income data.

In contrast to a widespread belief among economists, the use of the net-transfer calculation provides an incidence, which is clearly in favor of the lower-income deciles. As noted above, the pattern of the net-transfer calculation depends to a great extent on the student representation effect. The student representation effect itself depends particularly on the general social stratification within and among the income deciles and on the selectivity of the educational system with respect to parents' incomes. Even if it is true that the processes of selection and allocation of students are more in favor of the upper income brackets (in support of the thesis of many economists), the so-called level effect may overcompensate this structural effect.

Furthermore, the assumption of a proportional revenue incidence (tax incidence) implies that a distributional-neutral situation could only be obtained if the share of students who descended rose proportionally to gross income. Consider for example two deciles with incomes of 2,500 and 5,000 currency units respectively, and a given distribution of the benefits proportional to the student distribution (i.e. if an income bracket enrolled $y\%$ of the entire students, it would also receive $y\%$ of the benefits). The net incidence can be zero for both only if the better-off household group enrolls twice as many students in higher education. Therefore, even if wealthier households enroll significantly more children, a regressive distributional impact still cannot be concluded.

Some strong assumptions (first of all, the proportional tax incidence) had to be made due to a lack of data. Bedau and Teichmann (1995) have shown that in 1994, the indirect tax regression in Germany did not cancel the progressivity of income taxation and that the whole tax system was slightly progressive. Therefore, it should be noted that our assumptions are conservative. Considering progressive taxation, the net incidence would be more in favor of the lower income brackets. The same is true for the use of the square-root scale, which concentrates the income more effectively than the modified OECD scale. Furthermore, since the Socio-Economic Panel defines a household that consists only of a student as an independent household, some households ended up being counted twice.

As we have described in subsection 3.1.4, two sources of data have been used, the GSOEP and the 15th Social Survey. In the latter, students are invited to give information on parents' income. Unfortunately, we cannot judge whether students tend to underestimate (or overestimate) their family income.

Part II

The Distributional Impact of Subsidies to Higher Education in the Long Run

4

Previous Related Literature

4.1 Some Preliminary Remarks on Methodology

It is interesting to note that almost all empirical studies are cross-sectional analyses. Since such an analysis provides snapshots of the incidence at particular points of time, they can be criticized due to the fact that they ignore the longitudinal dimension of the point at issue. This critique also applies to the distributional effect of higher-education subsidies. In analyzing that effect, we have to distinguish between an analysis of children from various household types and an analysis of educated and non-educated individuals going through their life cycle. For the former, a cross-sectional examination is the only possibility; for the latter, a long-run analysis might be helpful. One question related to longitudinal analysis that needs to be addressed is whether or not graduates actually *pay back* their received benefits from public subsidization within their lifetime (see, for example, Grüske (1994) and confer also the discussion in Chapter 4.2). Another related question is how public higher education affects the income inequality in subsequent years.

The non-empirical literature often ignores the longitudinal-cross-sectional distinction and deals with a mixture of both views. Basically, a long-run analysis does not yield a distributional effect among *rich* and *poor* (cf. Grüske (1994), (Sturn and Wohlfahrt, 1999, ch. 6.1.3.3) and Barbaro (2001)). A relationship to such a socioeconomic variable is possible if a strong under-representation of students from socioeconomically disadvantaged backgrounds in higher education could be ascertained. Then, one can argue that students from higher-income families benefit the most from the subsidies and that those fortunate enough to get their higher education subsidized will receive all the returns from the human-capital investment, but the costs would be borne by all taxpayers, including the poorer ones. As we have seen, there is no evidence – at least for Germany – to support such a conclusion.

One of the most cited empirical work concerning the long-run effects is, again, Grüske (1994), whose study includes both a cross-sectional analysis and a long-run approach. The study became of policy concern, after some policy advise with reference to it has been put forth. For instance, in his paper commissioned by the *Sachverständigenrat* (German Council of Economic Advisers, see the footnote on page 14), Richter (1999) recommended a deep reform of the higher-education funding system in Germany also with regard to the unwanted distributional effects, as they have been pointed out by Grüske. Moreover, recent (German) reform proposals toward fees, vouchers, and loans (e.g. Ziegele et al. (1998); Bareis et al. (1999), and Sachverständigenrat Bildung (1998)) support their argumentation with the results of Grüske explicitly.[1] Hence, it seems to be worthwhile to speculate on this examination, in particular on the methodology. This is what the following Chapter 4.2 aims to do. The main goal by doing so is to critically assess the methodology of the study.

4.2 Grüske's Long-Run Analysis

4.2.1 Method

In this examination, the difference between the education-related tax payments of the former student during her working life and the received benefits during the time a student obtained higher education is calculated. The analysis considers only male students (cf. Grüske, 1994, p. 101).

The received benefits represent – similar to the cross-sectional analysis – 60% of university expenditures, which equal 2% of the whole tax revenue. If the received benefits during the period of higher education exceed the later return flow, we can observe a net benefit, which Grüske cites as an indication for redistribution.

Grüske restricts the examination design considerably when he stresses: "External effects and broader dynamic incidence effects due to adjustment reactions are neglected." (Grüske, 1994, p. 73) (own translation).

4.2.2 Results

In his examination, Grüske studied five groups of subjects. It was possible to obtain a positive net benefit for all of them. Table 4.1 provides the net benefits per students and with respect to the department.

These values are not discounted to the present value. Thus, academics carry between 24% and 40% of their costs of education themselves. "If the different time of usage and pay-back burden is taken into consideration and both figures are discounted to the present value, this portion falls to between 10% to 20%. To put it differently, a person without tertiary education and with

[1] At the time of writing, the current issue of the German weekly journal *Die Zeit* also refers to this study and presents table 4.1 on page 41 with the main results of the examination in order to illustrate the regressive distributional effects.

faculty	net benefit in DM
Medicine	123,000
Mathematics / Natural Sciences	92,000
Engineering	67,500
Languages and Cultural Sciences	57,700
Economics and Social Sciences	45,100

Table 4.1. Net benefit values, reported by Grüske

a significantly lower lifetime income carries up to 90% of the costs of higher education. In the life cycle, a redistribution from "below to above" can unambiguously be observed—contrasting the cross-section analysis, which only considers the origin of the students!" (Grüske, 1994, p. 283) (own translation).

4.2.3 Discussion

Assigning the Received Benefits

As mentioned above, 60% of university expenditures are assigned as subsidies whereas Grüske does not explain this value.

At the onset, it shall be pointed out that German universities are characterized by a unity of teaching and research. "Thus, the result is the allocation of a basic equipment for the university which is not divided into research and teaching. Even in the accounts of the universities [...], no difference between research and teaching is made" (Wissenschaftsrat, 1997, p. 32) (own translation). In order to quantify the proportion of resources devoted to research (henceforth: *research proportion*), several methods have been developed. However, the *Wissenschaftsrat* refers to the fact that "none of the methods [...] permits it to calculate the research proportion reliably. On the contrary, the methods only suggest an illusory accuracy" (ibid; own translation). The values which are the results of the several methods have a high variance. It is a simple way just to add 50% to both research and teaching. Although this method does not lead to actual proportions it, "does not delude a wrong accuracy." (Wissenschaftsrat, 1997, p. 32) (own translation).

Moreover, regarding all university expenditures as expenditures for traditionally expected responsibilities of universities (i.e. research and teaching) is rather problematic. For instance, in Germany, 51% of all university expenditures amounting to 30,773 million DM stem from the medical institutions.[2] Parts of these expenditures are pure health expenditures, which to a large extent would accrue even if the hospitals were not university hospitals. Therefore, it might be appropriate to exclude the medical sector from examinations like these.

[2] Data for 1998; source: (bmbf, 1999b, section 7). See also Barbaro and Wohlfahrt (1999).

Including the Repayment

Grüske attempts to answer the question whether or not academics carry the costs of their degree (cf. Grüske, 1994, p. 277). He therefore determines with regard to the principle of non-affectation 2% of all tax payments as repayments. However, using this method can lead to several problems:

(a) In spite of a complete repayment, the education choice may worsen the social welfare level compared to alternative choices.
Consider a social-sciences student as an example. The high number of social-science students has led to low average costs of graduation. For instance, despite having finished the graduation in social science, the student cannot find an appropriate job. However, if he had not earned a degree in the social sciences field then perhaps he would have become a banker (alternative choice).
Even if he might be able to *pay back* the received benefits with 2% of his tax payments, his education choice still leads to lower tax revenues, assuming that he earned more as a banker. To put it differently, his educational choice causes other individuals to be worse off, although redistribution in Grüske's sense has not occurred. On the contrary, a former medical student and present doctor is not able to pay back the high costs of his degree despite his higher tax burden. Indirectly, these doctors cause the non-academics to become better-off due to a higher income and higher tax payments. In this case, redistribution in Grüske's sense has occurred.

(b) A problematic concept of justice is applied.
Grüske does not distinguish between redistribution and justice. The case where academics do not generate a net benefit from their higher education is sufficient to conclude a just situation. On the other hand, a high income disparity between academics and non-academics might occur due to the respective level of education which might be regarded as unjust and which might be concerned with a lower social welfare.

(c) The way of adding the repayments is problematic from a tax-systematic point of view.
Grüske attempts to determine whether academics pay back the costs of their degree. Thus, received benefits are understood to be credits, and the repayment is determined by the general tax liability. As a consequence, a part of the tax payments is not declared as such (since it is a loan or credit repayment). This violates both, the principle of non-affectation and, through the linkage of received benefits and tax burden, also the *ability-to-pay* principle which only aims at the revenue side of the budget. If such a procedure is nevertheless applied, it infringes upon the postulate of horizontal tax equity: A non-graduate with identical tax payments will object that his tax payments are higher although the ability to pay is the same.

(d) The methodological procedure inevitably leads to a system in which academics cannot finance universities on their own.

It does not become entirely clear what Grüske really wants to show. If he is concerned with the question of whether or not non-graduates should have to take part in the financing of higher education, then the result is determined by the procedure. According to Grüske, the education-related university expenditures are financed by 2% of all tax revenues. Thus, this 2% consist of 2% of the graduate's tax payments and 2% of the tax payments of non-graduates. Therefore, it applies:

$$L = \alpha T_A + \alpha T_V; \qquad \alpha \in [0,1] \subset \mathbb{R}$$

where L represents the education-related university spending and α denotes the share of the entire tax revenue which is spent for L. T represents the tax payments of the graduates (subscript A) and non-academics (subscript V). The time index is neglected. Without further rearrangements, the equation shows that graduates can only finance the universities on their own if non-academics pay no taxes. A repayment in Grüske's sense is only possible if the real expenditures for university teaching rise sharply or if α increases steadily. In the first case, L has to rise steadily in all periods t, so that a complete repayment can be achieved:

$$L_t - L_{t-1} \overset{!}{=} \alpha\, T_{V,t}.$$

If the university expenditures are constant, this is impossible. Even if a repayment by graduates occurs, non-graduates still have to pay for the universities. Apparently, Grüske is aware of this problem since he writes with regard to his approach: "In order to determine the real growth rates which are at least required so that graduates pay back the received benefits through their university-related contributions, a *dynamic approach* is calculated for the group with the smallest net benefits: economists and social scientists. Thus, at least an unrealistic 5% real growth per year is required so that the graduates of these groups finance their received benefits by themselves" (Grüske, 1994, p. 120) (own translation). However, Grüske apparently does not recognize this fact as a weakness of his approach, but as confirmation of his distribution thesis.
The natural end of the second case occurs if the overall tax payments are used as education-related university expenditures ($\alpha = 1$).

(e) The repayment is not independent of the budget structure.
It has been mentioned in (*d*) that the repayment also depends on the share α. From a theoretical point of view, it is not to assume that the size of the repayment should depend on how the government handles transferred resources. On the contrary, it is crucial that resources flow from graduates to the public budget and from there (also) to the group of non-graduates. Additionally, a single graduate has practically no influence on the structure of public expenditures. If the university budget rises more sharply than the overall budget, an academic pays back more. If the university budget is, on the other hand, considerably reduced, the repayment

is smaller. This is the case although the overall tax payments remain unchanged. However, the overall tax payments and their distribution have an impact on the welfare respectively the income of non-academics as well.

4.2.4 Conclusion and Consequences

The critique expressed in item (*d*) is concerned with the realization of Grüske's examination. However, the points (*a*) and (*b*) express the basic demands on such a investigation. Only in a case where a group of persons is worse-off due to public higher-education funding, redistribution can be ascertained. Despite this problem, however, the procedure proposed by Grüske has been often accepted in the related literature. For instance, García-Peñalosa and Wälde (2000) put forth that:

> If the average tax payer has a lower lifetime income than the average university graduate [...], a subsidy to higher education financed from general taxation implies reverse lifetime redistribution, i.e. redistribution from the poor to the rich.

This is a good example for what has been mentioned above. The literature often confuses results obtained from cross-sectional analyses and those from longitudinal ones. Moreover, it is not clear why a lower lifetime income is sufficient to conclude a redistribution of income.

Public subsidization will probably have an impact on the distribution of income and wealth, but obviously, a new distribution is not necessarily concerned with *re*distribution. If public activity encourages economic growth, it cannot be said that the taxes raised in order to finance the subsidies have been squeezed out of anybody for others to benefit from. Indeed, as Musgrave and Musgrave (1984) pointed out, in discussing the incidence of various fiscal activities, in the longer run, the distributional impact will depend on the resulting effects of factor supplies, rates of return, and growth (cf. Musgrave and Musgrave, 1984, p. 678). Despite these remarks, investments in education may increase income dispersion in subsequent years as Mincer (1958) has shown in his seminal paper.

4.3 Johnson's Seminal Paper

An important work on the distributional effects of public higher education has been provided by Johnson (1984). He considers three groups: those who are talented enough to attend college (consisting of two subgroups) and those who are not capable of benefiting (directly) from college attendance. Members of the latter group are destined to remain low-skilled workers throughout their lifetimes but also can vote over the extent to which higher education is subsidized. Members of the former group can attend college, but do not necessarily do so. As a consequence, members of the first high-skilled group become high-skilled or medium-skilled workers.

Johnson demonstrates that in certain circumstances the low-skilled agents prefer a higher subsidy to higher education than the more talented do. In other words, he demonstrates that subsidizing higher education might be to the mutual interest of both the unskilled and the skilled workers. If this is the case, it cannot be said that the most talented agents receive subsidies at the expense of the unskilled workers—hence the result contradicts the reproach that subsidies are inequitable in the sense that those who will become more successful in labor market force less successful agents to pay for their investment in higher education so that the latter group is worse off. Due to the importance of this work for the ongoing discussion, we briefly summarize this paper and emphasize the most interesting results.

Johnson demonstrates that it is not a priori clear which of the groups wants a higher subsidy to higher education, because it depends on the nature of the aggregate production function and the parameters of the tax system.

Johnson distinguishes three groups of individuals. The first group has an innate ability to attend higher education and they do so. A second group consists of those who have also the requisite intelligence and sophistication to attend higher education, but abstain from doing so. The first group, whose size is denoted by L_h, become high-skilled workers whereas members of the second group, whose size is denoted by L_m, become medium-skilled workers. Members of the third group, whose size is L_u, are not capable of attending higher education and thus, they remain low-skilled workers throughout their lives. It is assumed that all persons work the same fixed number of hours during their lifetime and that this fixed number is not affected by the tax and transfer system.

The production process of the economy is that aggregate output, ν, is a linear-homogenous function of the three types of labor,

$$\nu = F\left(L_u, L_m, L_h\right), \tag{4.1}$$

where $F_i > 0$, $i \in \{u, m, h\}$ and $F_{ii} < 0$. The wages (w_i) are determined by $w_i = F_i$ and $\sum_i w_i \cdot L_i = \nu$ applies (Euler-Theorem).

A government is assumed to influence educational activities in two ways. First, it may subsidize the direct costs of obtaining higher education, c, by a rate of subsidization denoted by ρ.[3] Second, it collects taxes in order to finance the subsidies—which amount to $\rho\, c\, L_h$—and to finance other governmental activities. Those capable of attending higher education will undertake the educational investment if the after-tax difference in earnings between high- and medium-skilled workers equals the private cost of obtaining higher education:

$$(1-t)(w_h - w_m) = (1-\rho)c. \tag{4.2}$$

[3] In this brief summary of Johnson's paper we sometimes use other symbols as in the original source in order to avoid confusions with symbols in the next chapters.

The distributional consequences of education subsidies depend on the nature of $F(\cdot)$, in particular, the incidence critically depends on the complementarities between the three kinds of labor inputs. A useful way to analyze the complementarities is to consider the *partial elasticity of complementarity (PEC)* between factors i and j. The PEC is defined as

$$C_{ij} = \frac{F_{ij}\nu}{F_i F_j}. \tag{4.3}$$

The factors i and j are complements in production if an exogenous increase in L_j increases w_i. The PEC in this case is positive. The case of particular interest is that in which L_u and L_m are perfect substitutes. In this case the low-skilled agents want a positive subsidy even if they have to pay for all of it and the high- and medium-skilled workers want a negative one. The basic intuition here is that "it is in their collective interest to restrict the supply of the more skilled labor aggregate" ((Johnson, 1984, p. 314)). Note that this intuition is similar to that provided by Fernandez and Rogerson (1995), to which we already referred to on page 31. However, it is straightforward to find an example where this result does not apply, for instance, when the production output is specified by a CES-function (see (Johnson, 1984, ch. III(i))).

4.4 Nash Bargaining, Time Inconsistency and Open Economies

An interesting examination which deals with the point at issue has been recently provided by Poutvaara and Kanniainen (2000). Their main question is whether it is in the interest of the non-graduates to subsidize students through the public budget. They approve this question in a model with positive externalities in education and complementarity in production between human capital and labor supplied by the low-ability individuals. The paper's aim is to study the possibility of a voluntary *social contract* benefiting all groups instead of a voting equilibrium where the minority (i.e. the high-skilled agents) is worse-off. The distribution of the gains created by such a social contract depends on the relative power, as the groups are engaged in Nash bargaining.

The intuition so far is the same as expressed by Baran and Sweezy (1966) and Johnson (1984). The distributional implications are not necessarily regressive because the agents can negotiate on the value added.

Hitherto, there is no reason why a social contract shall not come off. However, a free-rider behavior of the low-skilled agents in an open economy may undermine such a contract. Their willingness to commit to an educational subsidy vanishes as they anticipate the inflow of educated agents from abroad when the domestic rate of return on education exceeds that abroad. In turn, the rational behavior of the educated will become socially inefficient as well due to the possibility of time inconsistency. This problem arises if the educated migrate because their after-tax income is higher abroad than domestically. The argument is similar to the large amount of literature on tax competition, hence it is not surprising that a main result of (Poutvaara and Kanniainen, 2000, p. 558) is that:

> The social contract of financing education between high- and low-ability individuals breaks down when the educated become mobile and social contracts are restricted to be national.

The main reason why we refer to this paper is that the basic needs which have been put forth in the discussion of the analysis of Grüske's study towards an analysis of the distributional effect among graduates and non-graduates have been considered here. What we will do in the next chapters is to make some attempt to address the question whether a social contract can really be established so easily.

However, the story can be told due to the assumption that every student creates an externality. This assumption is often made in the literature on the economics of education but it is also often criticized. Nevertheless, if (positive) externalities are created by subsidies to higher-education, it is not surprising that everybody can become better-off.

In the next chapter we will neglect the role of externalities and focus exclusively on the role of tax distortions and countervailing subsidies. Furthermore, we will also consider that in reality agent's abilities are hidden so that public policy cannot discriminate among them. Our analysis takes place in a model of higher education which has been developed by Creedy and François (1990). We will present some basic structures of the model and highlight some points which can be criticized. Building up on this model, we will use an extended and amended version of it to deal with the distributional effect of public subsidization in the long-run, i.e. we ask whether non-graduates are likely to become better off if higher-education investments are subsidized so that such subsidies to higher education are Pareto-superior.

5

The Creedy–François Model of Higher-Education Economics as the Basic Framework for our Analysis

Creedy and François (1990) developed a framework in which the following analysis takes place. The framework is a two-period cohort model with heterogeneous agents who endogenously decide on higher education with respect to taxation and subsidization. Higher education is the only investment good. An individual's choice of higher education depends in particular on its exogenously given endowment. Agents' income is taxed by a constant tax rate, and part of the direct costs of obtaining higher education is subsidized, where ρ denotes the rate of subsidization.

5.1 The Educational Choice of Individuals

A population of heterogeneous individuals who differ with respect to individual ability characteristics (endowments), denoted by y_i, is assumed. These endowments are crucial for the individual productivity and for the decision in favor or against pursuing a university degree. Two periods are considered. In the first period, each individual faces the decision whether to persue a degree or, alternatively, to start working as non-educated. In the second period, all individuals work. An individual chooses higher education if her net-lifetime earnings with a university degree exceed the lifetime earnings in case that she does not invest in higher education. The degree causes direct (and non tax-deductible) costs, c, for each individual. The total costs consist of the direct costs (e.g. teaching aids, tuition fees) and the foregone earnings. *Basic* incomes equal the individual endowment, y_i. Students have the opportunity to work even in the first period and, thus, earn the portion h of the income earned without higher education. Therefore, the total costs of obtaining higher education amount to

$$(1 - h)y_i + c. \tag{5.1}$$

Individuals who have completed a degree in the first period will raise their income in the second period due to the rate of return to education. To simplify matters, it is assumed that the individual rate of return to education, s_i, is proportional to the individual endowment:

$$s_i \equiv u \cdot y_i. \tag{5.2}$$

As noted above, in the first period each individual faces the decision whether to persue a degree or, alternatively, to start working without a university degree. The share's size of those choosing higher education depends on the exogenously given distribution of y.

It is assumed that graduates cause an externality benefiting (also) non-graduates, because this externality, denoted by g, raises all incomes. Furthermore, it is assumed that g depends on the graduation rate, denoted by p, and by an exogenously given parameter,[1] $\vartheta \in \mathbb{R}_{++}$, specified as

$$g = \vartheta \frac{p}{1+p}, \tag{5.3}$$

so that g increases from zero, when no investment in human capital takes place, to $0.5\,\vartheta$ if all agents invest in higher education. ϑ, however, is exogenously given.

The lifetime earnings of educated agents, V^E, and the lifetime earnings of non-educated ones, V^N are given by

$$V_i^E \equiv h\,y_i - c(1-\rho) + \frac{y_i(1+s_i+g)(1-t)}{1+r} \tag{5.4}$$

and

$$V_i^N \equiv y_i + \frac{y_i\,(1+g)\,(1-t)}{1+r} \tag{5.5}$$

where $r \in \mathbb{R}_{++}$ represents the discount rate. It is possible to find an ability level corresponding to that of an agent who is indifferent to investing in higher education, by setting (5.4)=(5.5). This ability level is defined to be *educational-choice margin (ECM)*, $\tilde{y}$. An individual i makes a decision in favor of higher education if her net-lifetime earnings as a graduate exceed those of being a non-graduate. This is the case if her endowment, y_i, exceeds the educational-choice margin.

As a consequence of this model, only those individuals with the highest endowment will be enrolled in higher education. The government can introduce a subsidy to higher education in order to (partially) cover the direct costs of higher education. $F(y)$ denotes the distribution function of y, so that it measures the proportion of individuals with endowments less than or equal to y. The proportion of individuals who invest in higher education is given by

$$p \equiv 1 - F(\tilde{y}). \tag{5.6}$$

[1] We use ϑ instead of δ in the original source.

5.2 Budget Constraint and Tax Base

The entire public expenditures consist of the grants to higher education and of non-education expenditures. The required revenue per capita in order to finance non-education expenditure is equal to the fixed amount R. The amount per individual which has to be raised through taxation is equal to Γ,[2] where

$$\Gamma = \rho c \left[1 - F(\tilde{y})\right] + R. \tag{5.7}$$

Let n denote the number of individuals in question. Then, total income in the first period of those with an endowment below the ECM is equal to

$$n \int_0^{\tilde{y}} y \, dF(y). \tag{5.8}$$

Those with an endowment above the ECM earn an income in the first period equal to their endowment minus the opportunity costs of higher education:

$$n \int_{\tilde{y}}^{\infty} hy \, dF(y). \tag{5.9}$$

Hence, total income in the first period amounts to:

$$n \left[\int_0^{\tilde{y}} y \, dF(y) + \int_{\tilde{y}}^{\infty} hy \, dF(y) \right]. \tag{5.10}$$

In the second period, non-graduates raise their income only through the external benefit, according to equation (5.5). Thus, total income of those below $\tilde{y}$ simply amounts to $\frac{(1+g)}{(1+r)}$ multiplied by (5.8). In contrast to those with $y_i < \tilde{y}$, the derivation of the total income of the graduates in the second period is more tedious. They raise their income due to both, the externality (like the non-graduates) and the private rentability[3] of their higher education. Furthermore, they obviously do not bear any longer the opportunity costs. Thus, raising the basic income (i.e. the income which equals the endowment) of the graduates due to the externality and due to the private rentability, yields:

$$n \frac{(1+g)}{(1+r)} \int_{\tilde{y}}^{\infty} y \, dF(y) + \frac{n \cdot u}{(1+r)} \int_{\tilde{y}}^{\infty} y^2 \, dF(y). \tag{5.11}$$

In the following chapters, we will amend this framework in order to illustrate our main points.

---

[2] We use Γ instead of R_t in the original source in order to avoid possible confusions with the required fixed amount R.

[3] With *private rentability* we denote the marketability of the higher-education investment.

5.3 A Critique of the Externalities in the Creedy-François-Model and the Role of Tax Distortions

5.3.1 The Role of Externalities

The normative justification of subsidies to education has been discussed for decades. In the last decades, advocates of public activities in the education sector have particularly referred to externalities, credit constraints, and distributional issues.[4] The discussion about externalities gained more importance in the 1980s and 1990s, particularly because of the seminal paper of Haveman and Wolfe (1984) and because of new developments in growth theory, following the dismissal of earlier explanations based on neoclassical marginal productivity theory (cf. Blaug, 1970, pp. 112ff). However, the empirical evidence for positive externalities is scant at best (see Acemoglu and Angrist, 2000; Bils and Klenow, 2000; Krueger and Lindahl, 2001) for recent contributions.

The importance of credit constraints is disputable as well. Capital-market imperfections, so the argument goes, may hinder poor agents financing the costs of obtaining higher education (see Saint-Paul and Verdier (1993); Perotti (1993); Benabou (2000, 2002)). However, there is little empirical evidence (see, e.g. Carneiro and Heckman (2002); Cameron and Heckman (2001); Keane and Wolpin (2001)). Friedman (1962) and others (see Epple and Romano (1998) for an overview) have persuasively argued that vouchers or student loans, for example, are a better means to compensate for unwanted effects that result from credit constraints. However, even if all classical arguments in favor of public subsidization cannot be dismissed as a whole, most economists argue that these arguments cannot justify the wide prevalence of education subsidies in many countries, in particular in Europe.

The justification which refers to externalities plays a crucial role. As noted above, it is hard to dismiss that higher education is concerned with positive externalities. However, there are two main problems.

First, it is not clear who and what precisely creates an external effect and furthermore, whether those creating an externality are really motivated to do so through unconditional grants. Fiscal activity often influences the behavior of some people rather than that of the whole population. As we will see in the next chapter, those with the highest ability will take up a degree independently of any fiscal activity.

Recent contributions see externalities created by R&D activities rather than by human capital in general (cf, for instance, Davidson and Segerstrom (1998) for a similar interpretation.). If those with the highest ability levels are those who are related to R&D after having completed a degree, it should be critically assessed whether the subsidization really makes a contribution to the creation of externalities. Such a creation can be explained if the graduation rate is very low and, hence, those who extrinsically invest in higher education

[4] See Barbaro (2003a) for a survey of empirical works on the issue.

(i.e. those who invest due to the subsidization) are those with the highest abilities.

Second, despite this large and persistent controversy, the quantification of the externalities remains problematic. If the externalities created by fiscal activities are sufficiently large, an extensive role of the state is almost always justified. To put if differently, almost every result is highly sensitive with respect to the assumed externality and its quantitative dimension. In the concrete example, a high ϑ (cf. equation (5.3)) can require and justify an extensive fiscal role and vice versa. Moreover, a high ϑ might hide some *structural problems* related to fiscal activities. For instance, the state can create externalities very inefficiently, but nevertheless, everybody ends up better-off due to the created growth.

While the first point is related to economic theory, the second point is more concerned with *technical* problems. However, a main critique with regard to the Creedy-François-Model (henceforth referred to as C-F-Model) and many other papers in the field of the economics of education (see Haveman and Wolfe (1984) for an overview) is its inclusion of the externality in the specified form expressed in equation (5.3). In this thesis, we neglect the existence of externalities. A justification for fiscal activities is given by a distortion created by income taxation.

5.3.2 The Role of Tax Distortions in the Recent Literature

While earlier discussions were centered around the expenditure side of the budget, recent[5] contributions focus more on revenue. The impact of taxes on human-capital accumulation has become the central element in the recent literature. Trostel (1993, 1996) has shown that taxation has a negative impact on human capital investments and that education subsidies should primarily be seen and justified as a compensation for this tax distortion. In making this argument, Trostel uses an econometric model with a proportional tax rate, and it is assumed that the direct costs of obtaining higher education are not tax-deductible.

Dupor et al. (1998) analyzed the distorting impact of progressive taxation based on US tax law in 1970. The findings show that progressivity led to an approximately 5-percent decline in human-capital investment in 1970. Based on data from 1990, the impact differed considerably depending on the choice of schooling, and lay between close to zero and −22%. Sturn and Wohlfahrt (2000) referred to the *foregone smoothing benefit*. Due to tax progression, combined with annual tax assessment, graduates pay more taxes than non-

[5] Previous examinations of the effect of taxation on human-capital accumulation are, e.g. Heckman (1976), and Eaton and Rosen (1980). In both works, labor-income taxation was found to have a neutral effect, but in both papers only the opportunity costs of obtaining higher education are considered.

graduates with the same net lifetime earnings because graduates accumulate their income in a shorter period of time.[6]

In summary, recent contributions have focused more on the inefficiencies created by taxation than on the externalities created by human-capital investment. In these recent papers and in previous examinations (Heckman (1976); Eaton and Rosen (1980)), investment in education is a continuous decision, i.e. homogenous agents optimize the time devoted to education. In practice, however, we observe that the investment decision in favor of higher education is made by some agents whereas others avoid higher education. In this paper, we show that equity effects of education subsidies differ remarkably if the educational-investment decision is discrete. The reason is that here the tax distortion affects only a fraction of the population instead of the whole, as in the aforementioned studies.

Our amended version of the C-F-model includes an inefficiency created by taxation which can be counteracted by subsidization. Such a subsidization also has a distributional dimension which we also address. Creedy and François create their model in a way which also allows the discussion of inefficiencies through income taxation although the authors do not discuss these effects explicitly, probably because the literatures which has (in particular) experienced a renaissance after the seminal works of Trostel (1996) and Dupor et al. (1998) has been published afterwards.

[6] In addition, Wigger (2004) supported the implications of the above research in the case where subsidies to higher education are combined with optimal linear income taxes à la Sheshinski (1972), but social welfare cannot be increased by supplementing a nonlinear income tax (in the tradition of Mirrless (1971)) with a subsidization of direct costs.

6

The Distributional Effect of Public Subsidization Among Graduates and Non-Graduates—The Life-Cycle Perspective

6.1 Introduction

In this chapter, we will use an amended version of the Creedy-François model in order to discuss our point. In our model, a tax is levied on agents' income, thereby assuming a constant tax rate to be exogenously given. The resulting revenue is spent on redistribution and subsidization purposes. Each agent receives an identical lump-sum transfer, whose amount depends on the tax base, the tax rate, and the amount of costs devoted to finance higher-education subsidies. At this point, the trade-off becomes evident. The more is spent to support higher education through an unconditional grant, the lower the proportion of the whole revenues devoted to redistribution. On the other hand, the tax base might be positively affected by subsidization so that two effects work in an opposite direction. If no subsidization takes place, however, the entire revenue is earmarked uniformly among all individuals.

Such a redistribution policy is progressive, because it rewards the low-ability agents while the mean earner neither gains nor loses in contrast to those with an income above the mean who are the losers. The assumption of a lump-sum transfer towards all agents simplifies the analysis, because it has no impact on the educational-choice margin.

In contrast to the lump-sum transfer, the effect of income taxation is twofold. It allows it to finance the described redistribution policy, but it distorts the choice between education and work in the first period. According to the recent literature (see Section 5.3), this distortion calls for efficiency-enhancing subsidies. The efficiency gains created by a (partial) subsidization are potentially Pareto superior.

This chapter is organized as follows. Section 6.2 presents a general framework in which our analysis is put forth. Section 6.3 discusses the distortionary effects of taxation and analyzes the amount of subsidization which is required to counteract the efficiency loss. Section 6.4 then deals with the question whether the efficiency gains can be used to compensate the non-graduates for their renouncement of a higher transfer and highlight the role of windfall profits.

6.2 The Model

To make our point, we use an amended version of the model presented by Creedy and François (1990). Their model consists of a population of agents who differ with respect to their innate endowment. It is a two-period model. In the first period, all agents face the decision of whether to enroll in a degree program or not. In the second period, all agents work, either as graduates or as non-graduates. The government is assumed to raise taxes. The entire public revenue is spent financing subsidies to higher education, and for a publicly-provided good. The graduation rate depends on the tax rate, the rate of subsidization, and on an externality created by those who attend higher education (see the preceding section).

Our framework differs from the model of Creedy and François (1990) in two respects. First, we neglect the existence of externalities. A justification for fiscal activities is given by a distortion created by income taxation according to the recent literature cited in Subsection 5.3.2. Secondly, in our model a tax is levied on agents' incomes, thereby assuming a constant tax rate to be exogenously given. The resulting revenue is spent on redistribution and subsidization purposes. Each agent receives an identical lump-sum transfer, denoted by $\aleph \in \mathbb{R}_+$, whose amount depends on the tax base, the tax rate, and the amount devoted to financing higher-education subsidies. At this point, a trade-off becomes evident. The more is spent to support higher education through an unconditional grant, the lower the proportion of all revenue devoted to the redistribution policy. On the other hand, the tax base might be positively affected by subsidization so that the two effects work in opposite directions. If no subsidization takes place, however, the entire revenue is distributed uniformly among all individuals.

In contrast to the lump-sum transfer, the effect of income taxation is twofold. It allows the described redistribution policy, but it distorts the choice between education and work in the first period. This distortion calls for efficiency-enhancing subsidies. The efficiency gains created by a (partial) subsidization are potentially Pareto-superior. We do not ask why a distortionary taxation exists. We instead assume that a non-distortionary tax system is politically not feasible, so that policy aim is to implement a second-best means to offset the distortion.

Assume that a population is heterogeneous with respect to the innate endowment $y_i \in [0, \hat{y}] \subset \mathbb{R}$. Population size is normalized to unity. As in Creedy and François (1990), we consider that the cohort lives in two periods. In the first period, each agent can choose between higher education and work. In the second period, the entire population works. An individual's gross income is determined by her individual innate endowment and her return from higher education (if obtained). The distribution of the initial endowments is represented by the twice differentiable density function, $f(y)$, and its corresponding distribution function, $F(y)$. A constant and exogenously given tax rate, $t \in [0, 1) \subset \mathbb{R}$, is levied on all income.

An individual chooses higher education if his or her net lifetime earnings with an university degree would exceed the lifetime earnings if he or she did not invest in higher education. The degree causes direct (and non tax-deductible) costs, $c \in \mathbb{R}_{++}$, for each individual, where a proportion $\rho \in [0, 1] \subset \mathbb{R}$ is borne by the taxpayers. The government knows only the distribution of the innate abilities, but cannot observe the endowment of each agent. Accordingly, the government can not establish individual-specific subsidies.

It is important to note that the costs of higher education, c, are not tax-deductible. The total costs, therefore, consist of the direct costs, such as teaching aids and tuition fees, and earnings foregone. *Basic* incomes equal the innate endowment, y_i. Students have the opportunity to work even in the first period and, thus, earn the portion $h \in [0, 1] \subset \mathbb{R}$ of the income earned without higher education. Therefore, the total cost of obtaining higher education amounts to

$$(1-h)y_i(1-t) + c(1-\rho). \tag{6.1}$$

Individuals who have completed a degree in the first period will raise their income in the second period because of the rate of return to education. To simplify matters, it is assumed that the individual rate of return to education, s_i, is proportional to the individual endowment:

$$s_i \equiv u\, y_i. \tag{6.2}$$

As noted above, in the first period each individual faces the decision of whether to enroll in a degree program or, alternatively, to start working without a university degree. The share of those choosing higher education depends on the exogenously given distribution of y.

The present values of the net lifetime income of educated agents, V^E, and of non-educated ones, V^N, are given by

$$V_i^E = (1-t)h\, y_i - c(1-\rho) + \frac{(1-t)\, y_i\, (1+u\, y_i)}{1+r} + \aleph \tag{6.3}$$

and by

$$V_i^N = (1-t)\, y_i + \frac{(1-t)\, y_i}{1+r} + \aleph. \tag{6.4}$$

It is straightforward to find an ability level corresponding to that of an agent who is indifferent to investing in his or her higher education by setting (6.3) = (6.4). The agent's endowment is denoted by $\tilde{y}$ and is henceforth referred to as the *educational-choice margin* (*ECM*). It is

$$\tilde{y}^{[p]} \equiv \psi + \sqrt{\psi^2 + \omega \cdot \frac{(1-\rho)}{(1-t)}} \tag{6.5}$$

where $\psi \equiv \frac{(1-h)(1+r)}{2u}$ and $\omega \equiv \frac{c}{u}(1+r)$.[1] We assume that agents behave atomistically, neglecting the impact of their investment on aggregate income and total tax revenue.

As can be seen, the lump-sum transfer has no impact on the educational-choice margin. This is because the lump-sum transfer is granted to both types of agents uniformly and, therefore, does not distort the choice of educational investment.

For the ongoing discussion, it is useful to define a benchmark equilibrium. For this, we take the non-interventionist, redistribution-free equilibrium, where the government does not implement any income policy, so that the educational-choice margin is fully determined by market forces. This benchmark case is determined by $\rho = t = 0$. The educational-choice margin is then given by

$$\tilde{y}^{[bm]} = \psi + \sqrt{\psi^2 + \omega}. \tag{6.6}$$

The second case considers a (flat) tax on income ($0 < t < 1$) and investments in higher education are not subsidized ($\rho = 0$). As noted above, we assume that the direct cost of obtaining higher education is not effectively tax-deductible. This assumption, which holds for a wide range of countries (see Trostel (1993)), is the driving force in Trostel (1993, 1996). In those papers, Trostel argues that a subsidy to higher education may be regarded as a means to compensate for the distorting nature of taxation. The educational-choice margin in this case is given by

$$\tilde{y}_0^{[p]} = \psi + \sqrt{\psi^2 + \frac{\omega}{(1-t)}}. \tag{6.7}$$

As can be seen, the higher t, the higher the educational-choice margin and, consequently, the lower the graduation rate. On the other hand, the educational-choice margin is lowered if part of the cost of obtaining higher education is borne by the state. This can be seen by comparing (6.5) and (6.7).

To assess the distortionary effects of taxation on educational choice careful differentiation between different groups of individuals has to be conducted. The first group consists of those agents with an innate endowment below $\tilde{y}^{[bm]}$. They would not invest in higher education in the benchmark case and would be even less likely to if a distorting tax system would be introduced. The proportion of these agents is henceforth denoted by $n_1 \equiv F\left(\tilde{y}^{[p]}\right)$. The second group consists of those agents who would invest in their higher education in the benchmark case, but are deterred from doing so because of the establishment of a distorting income tax. A subsidy is then required to give them an

[1] As $V^{[E]}$ slopes quadratically, there is a second solution. It is given by $\psi - \sqrt{\psi^2 + \omega \cdot \frac{(1-\rho)}{(1-t)}}$. As ω, ρ, and t are all nonnegative, and $0 \leq \rho \leq 1$, $0 \leq t < 1$, this second solution is negative because the square root exceeds ψ. Hence, (6.5) is unique in the relevant range. See Appendix G.1 for a derivation.

incentive to correct their investment decision. If agents invest in higher education because of a government compensation for existing distortions, then we call this decision *extrinsic*. We denote the fraction of agents investing in higher education extrinsically by $n_2 \equiv F\left(\tilde{y}_0^{[p]}\right) - n_1$. For the third group of agents, it is worthwhile investing in higher education although this investment is discouraged by income taxation. Their investment is said to be *intrinsically* motivated. The fraction of agents investing intrinsically is denoted by $n_3 \equiv 1 - n_1 - n_2$. $\bar{y}_j$ with $j \in \{1, 2, 3\}$ denoting the mean endowment of agents in group j, and $V(y_j)$ the variance of their innate endowments.

In the next section, we will analyze the combined effect of taxation and subsidization of human-capital formation. By doing so, we derive the condition for efficiency-enhancing subsidies given the existence of the distorting nature of taxation.

6.3 Subsidization and Efficiency

Starting from the benchmark case ($\rho = t = 0$), there would be no potential for Pareto improvement through the establishment of public education. As there are no tax distortions or other market failures, the outcome is Pareto optimal. Subsidization financed by a non-distorting tax[2] would always lead to a *re*distribution.

The more reasonable case, however, is that where a distorting income tax is imposed. Hence, starting from $\tilde{y}_0^{[p]}$, we are interested in the effect of various ρ-values on the educational-choice margin. In particular, we wish to infer the optimal rate of subsidization if $\tilde{y}_0^{[p]}$ equals the educational-choice margin in the benchmark case, $\tilde{y}^{[bm]}$. The subsidy to higher education is said to be efficient (Pareto-improving) if it leads to increased aggregate income.

Proposition 6.1. *Under proportional taxation, a fiscal activity, which consists of the combination of revenue and spending policy, is optimal if the rate of subsidization equals the tax rate. If the rate of subsidization exceeds the tax rate, the educational-choice margin falls and p rises. In the opposite case, p falls if* $\frac{\rho}{t} < 1$.

Proof. If $\frac{\rho}{t} = 1$, it follows that the term $\frac{(1-\rho)}{(1-t)} = 1$ and, hence, $\tilde{y}^{[p]} = \psi + \sqrt{\psi^2 + \omega} = \tilde{y}^{[bm]}$. See also Appendix G.2. □

---

[2] Optimal-tax theory states that the optimal tax is a lump-sum tax (see e.g. Eaton and Rosen, 1980, p. 706). We can prove that a lump-sum tax, denoted by τ, does not influence the educational-choice margin: The present value of a graduate's lifetime income is given by $hy_i - c + \frac{y_i(1+s_i)}{1+r} - \tau$ and that of a non-graduate by $y_i\left(1 + \frac{1}{1+r}\right) - \tau$. By equating both, the resulting educational-choice margin is independent of τ.

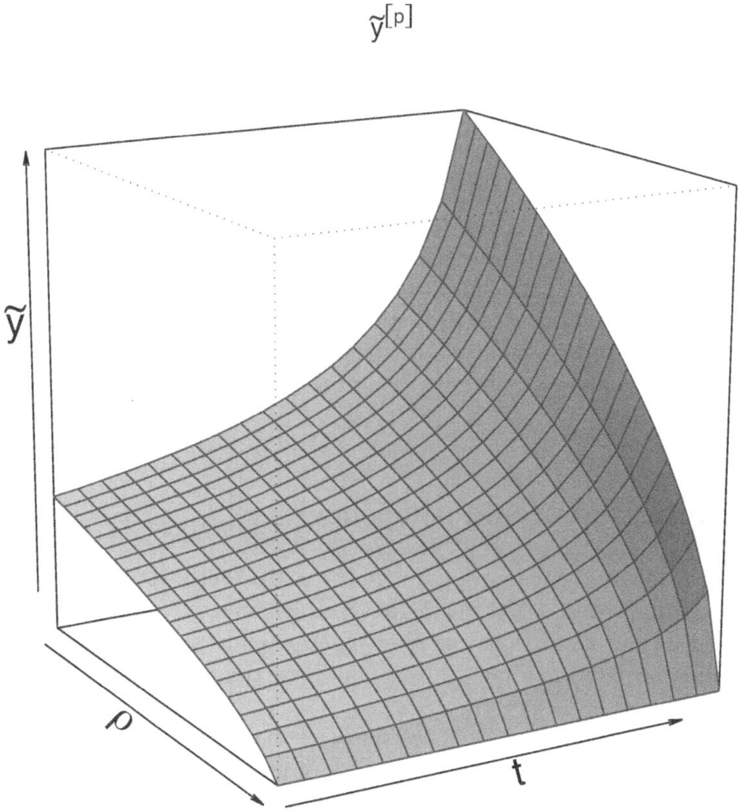

Fig. 6.1. $\tilde{y}^{[p]}$ for various ρ- and t-values

Figure 6.1 shows the *ECMs* that result from various ρ- and t-values. As can be seen along the ρ-axis, the higher the rate of subsidization, the lower the educational-choice margin. The opposite holds for the tax rate, except for one special case. This special case arises if the costs of obtaining higher education are totally borne by the government.

Proposition 6.2. *If the direct costs of obtaining higher education are completely borne by the state* ($\rho = 1$), *t has no effect on p.*

Proof. If $\rho = 1$, it follows that $\tilde{y}^{[p]} = 2\psi = \frac{(1-h)(1+r)}{u}$ and, thus, is independent of t. □

The intuition is as follows: The only distortion in this simple case of a proportional tax system arises from the non-deductibility of the direct cost of obtaining higher education. However, if the direct costs of higher education are completely borne by the state, the distortionary effect of non-deductibility does not play any role, because in that case the agents would have nothing to deduct.

Optimality implies that aggregate net lifetime earnings—the sum of the net lifetime earnings of those who do and those who do not invest in higher education—are maximized when subsidization completely countervails the tax distortion. As we do not consider any disincentives from taxation on the labor market (i.e. substitution effects on leisure) in our framework, aggregate net lifetime income equals aggregate gross income minus the aggregate costs of obtaining higher education. We denote aggregate income by W, so that

$$\begin{aligned} W = \left(1 + \frac{1}{1+r}\right) \int_{0}^{\tilde{y}} y\, dF(y) + \frac{1}{1+r} \int_{\tilde{y}}^{\hat{y}} y\, dF(y) \\ + \frac{u}{1+r} \int_{\tilde{y}}^{\hat{y}} y^2\, dF(y) + h \int_{\tilde{y}}^{\hat{y}} y\, dF(y) - c(1 - F(\tilde{y})). \end{aligned} \tag{6.8}$$

Here, for simplicity, we denote $\tilde{y}^{[p]}$ by $\tilde{y}$. Differentiating W with respect to the rate of subsidization yields

$$\tilde{y}(\rho) \cdot \tilde{y}'(\rho)\, f(\tilde{y} \left[1 - u\tilde{y}\,\frac{1}{1+r} - h\right] + c\, f(\tilde{y}) \cdot \tilde{y}'(\rho) = 0. \tag{6.9}$$

As a first order condition we derive $\rho = t$.

Proof. Differentiating W with respect to ρ yields eq. (6.9) $\Leftrightarrow$

$$\tilde{y}'\, f(\tilde{y}) \left[\tilde{y}(1-h) - \tilde{y}^2 \frac{u}{(1+r)+c}\right] = 0$$

$$\Leftrightarrow$$

$$\tilde{y}(1-h) - \tilde{y}^2 \frac{u}{(1+r)+c} = 0$$

The solution set, denoted by $\mathbb{L}$, is given by $\mathbb{L} = \{\psi + \sqrt{\psi^2 + \omega}\}$ □

The fact that a rate of subsidization up to t raises aggregate income implies that subsidies may be Pareto-improving. It is potentially feasible to distribute the efficiency gains so that all agents, including the non-graduates, are better off, although non-graduates have not benefited directly from subsidization. As noted in Section 4.3, Johnson (1984) argues that non-graduates' incomes may (also) be increased in such a manner, so that subsidization is *equitable*. In the next section, therefore, we will go into in more detail about the equity effects of subsidies to higher education. We will show that there is a counterforce that limits the distributive virtues of subsidies to education.

6.4 Subsidization and Equity: Are Subsidies Pareto-Improving?

A funding scheme is said to be equitable if all groups increase their net lifetime income due to subsidization. Otherwise, non-graduates are worse off and a redistribution from non-graduates to graduates has occurred. In the latter case, we can ascertain an equity-efficiency trade-off. Note also that subsidies may be potentially Pareto-improving if they are not equitable (i.e. lowering the net lifetime income of the non-graduates). If such subsidies raise net lifetime income of all agents, then equity-efficiency harmony exists. In this case, subsidization is said to be Pareto-superior.

Equity, therefore, requires raising the income of each of the three groups.[3] To verify whether subsidies achieve this, we treat each group in succession for the case $\rho = t$.[4] By doing so, we distinguish three kinds of income: gross income, net income (gross income minus taxes), and disposable income, i.e. net income plus the lump-sum transfer minus the cost of obtaining higher education (if obtained). The most important of these is disposable income. As we set the tax rate exogenously and constant, a rising gross income implies a rising net income and vice versa.

- GROUP 1. The gross income of group-1 agents (non-graduates) remains unchanged as does their net income. The only effect they experience is a change in $\aleph$. As total revenue is spent on redistribution and subsidization, the introduction of a subsidy leads to a twofold effect on $\aleph$. In the first period, a direct and an indirect effect occur. The direct effect on $\aleph$ results from the obvious fact that a proportion of the entire revenue is now spent for subsidization rather than for the lump-sum transfer alone. The indirect effect results from the fact that group-2 agents earn less in the first period than otherwise (opportunity costs of obtaining higher education) and therefore pay less in taxes.
  Formally, total costs per capita of the subsidies are given by

$$C(\rho, \tilde{y}(\rho)) \equiv p \cdot \rho c + t\,(1-h) \int y\, dF(y) \tag{6.10}$$

  where the limits of integration are given by $\tilde{y}^{[bm]}$ and $\tilde{y}_0^{[p]}$.
  The first term of the right-hand side of equation (6.10) features the change in the expenditure side of the budget. A part of the total revenue is now spent for subsidization rather than for redistribution alone. The decline in tax revenues in the first period, caused by the indirect costs of obtaining higher education, is represented by the second term.

[3] Here we follow (Sinn, 1995, p 497), who clearly distinguished between *equity* and *equitable*. As he said, "equity is an aspect of efficiency". For the concept of *equality* see Haveman (1988).

[4] Note that in this case $n_1 = 1 - F(\tilde{y}^{[bm]})$.

While the non-graduates face costs in the first period, they benefit from subsidization in the second period. The intuition is that they will also participate in the private rentability of human-capital investments through taxation and the use of the additional tax revenues for a higher lump-sum transfer. On the other hand, only a small portion of the taxed benefits from the private rentability of the investment could be assigned as benefits from the non-graduates' point of view. The private rentability of those who invest intrinsically would otherwise (i.e. without subsidization) also be taxed, so that only the tax revenue from the additional income of *group-2 agents* could be assigned as a benefit from subsidization. Formally, the benefit function (per capita) is $B(\tilde{y}(\rho))$, where

$$B(\tilde{y}(\rho)) \equiv t \cdot \frac{u}{(1+r)} \int y^2 \, dF(y), \tag{6.11}$$

and the same limits of integral as in (6.10) apply. Note that the effect on $\aleph$ is the same for all agents, as the lump-sum transfer is earmarked to be shared uniformly among all agents.

Again, it is crucial to note that group-1 agents are better off only if $\aleph$ rises due to subsidization, because the second source of their disposable income, net income, remains unchanged in both cases, with and without subsidization.

- GROUP 2. In contrast to group-1 agents, subsidization affects both income sources of group-2 agents, net income as well as $\aleph$. Nevertheless, we can easily show that group-2 agents are net gainers from the subsidy. These agents consist of those who change their investment decision after a subsidy has been established. Their reason is that they find it worthwhile investing in their education because of the subsidy. This means that the present value of their lifetime income is higher as a graduate than as a non-graduate.
- GROUP 3. As noted above, group-3 agents' investment in education is motivated intrinsically. They would invest in education even if the government did not counteract tax distortions. As a consequence, group-3 agents receive the same gross income (and the same net income) as without subsidization. Hence, they reap the subsidies as a pure windfall gain. They are therefore net gainers as long as $\rho c + \Delta\aleph > 0$ applies.

In summary, a subsidy to higher education affects the educational choices of group-2 agents. Group-3 agents, on the other hand, reap pure windfall gains. Such windfall gains may have a lowering effect on $\aleph$ because they lower the fraction of total revenue that is devoted to financing the lump-sum transfer. We obtain, therefore, the following Proposition:

Proposition 6.3. *A subsidy that is granted to each agent who invests in higher education intrinsically reduces the lump-sum transfer by* ρc.

In contrast to the effect of subsidizing group-3 agents, the subsidies to group-2 agents have a positive effect on $\aleph$. Formally, we obtain the following Proposition:

Proposition 6.4. *If all agents with an endowment below $\tilde{y}_0^{[p]}$ and above the efficient level $\tilde{y}^{[bm]}$ are subsidized by $\rho \cdot c$ and no other agent is subsidized, then $\aleph$ rises.*

We can prove Proposition 6.4 as follows:

Proof. For an individual whose endowment y_i is equal to $\tilde{y}^{[bm]}$, as a consequence of Proposition 6.1, the following equality applies:

$$u\,y_i^2\,\frac{1-t}{1+r} = (1-h)y_i(1-t) + (1-\rho)\,c, \quad \text{with} \quad \rho = t. \tag{6.12}$$

The left-hand side of equation (6.12) measures the additional net lifetime income (in present value terms) due to the investment in higher education, and the right-hand side measures the total costs of obtaining higher education, consisting of the direct and indirect costs of obtaining higher education. We can now multiply both sides by $\frac{t}{(1-t)}$ to obtain an equation whose left-hand side yields the additional tax revenues and consequently raising $\aleph$, and whose right-hand side indicates foregone tax revenues in the first period plus the expenditures for subsidizing this individual:

$$t \cdot \frac{u\,y_i^2}{(1+r)} = t\,[(1-h)\,y_i + c]\,. \tag{6.13}$$

Equation (6.13) states that it has no effect on $\aleph$ if an individual with an endowment equal to $\tilde{y}^{[bm]}$ is subsidized by $\rho \cdot c$. All individuals with higher endowments, however, will find it worthwhile to invest in higher education so that (6.12) becomes an inequality with its left-hand side exceeding its right-hand. The opposite case holds for all individuals with an endowment below $\tilde{y}^{[bm]}$.

It is now simple to consider all individuals with an endowment below $\tilde{y}_0^{[p]}$ by generalizing equations (6.12) and (6.13) to

$$u\,y_i^2\,\frac{1-t}{1+r} \lesseqqgtr (1-h)y_i(1-t) + (1-\rho)\,c, \quad \forall\, y_i \lesseqqgtr \tilde{y}^{[bm]} \tag{6.14}$$

and

$$t \cdot \frac{u\,y_i^2}{(1+r)} \lesseqqgtr t\,[(1-h)\,y_i + c]\,, \quad \forall\, y_i \lesseqqgtr \tilde{y}^{[bm]}. \tag{6.15}$$

Only the case in the bottom line of equation (6.15) is concerned with an increasing $\aleph$. □

In summary, we have seen that each subsidized group-2 agent contributes to an increasing lump-sum transfer and affects the disposable income of each group-1 agent positively. The opposite applies to each subsidized group-3 agent.

7

Alternative Options for Funding

Over the recent decades, the pros and cons of various kinds of higher-education funding have been discussed. In this section, we will discuss some of the proposals for a funding reform in the light of our framework and the main results we have obtained so far.

In the preceding sections we emphasized the role of tax distortions. We ignored the role of externalities and we made no attempt to address the role of capital-market imperfections or unequal opportunity to access higher education. The persistent debate on alternative funding options, however, often tries to consider most of these problems and to look for alternative funding schemes that alleviate or solve all or most of these problems.

Among others, the most popular ideas for a funding reform are: a graduate tax, vouchers, differential fees, and loans (see, e.g. Greenaway and Haynes (2003)). Most of these are mutually compatible in the sense that they work in a similar manner. Both vouchers and loans aim to correct market failures such as credit constraints. However, both schemes intend that graduates repay support received during their lifetime. A graduate tax is a mechanism to differentiate with respect to a concept, often weakly defined, of *ability to pay*; differential fees have a similar aim. However, only a small minority of economists claim that grants should be wholly state financed. The opposite attitude, however, seems to interest more economists, but two main drawbacks are also widely accepted. The first is concerned with equity considerations: tuition fees have become a target of much social hostility, mainly because they have to be paid at a time when young people have the least money. The second disadvantage is concerned with efficiency: considering the first drawback, parental contributions become more and more important and, despite the suggestion that this might also be socially undesirable, it separates payers (parents) and users (students). Consequently, so the argument goes, higher education is not an efficient decision because of a principal-agent problem.

Furthermore, this divergence of payers and users may be the source of what John Stuart Mill labeled *fiscal illusion.*[1]

Therefore, the debate within the economics of education is centered on a scheme somewhere between fully subsidized costs of obtaining higher education and tuition fees in its rough form. The main question in this field seems to be the relationship between the benefit granted during the investment period and the amount of *repayment* over the subsequent lifetime. The options here can be summarized as

- a pure (mortgage-type) loan scheme,
- a loan with income-related repayment (up to the borrowed amount), and
- a graduate tax.

Under a loan scheme, a graduate repays what he or she has borrowed until the loan (plus interest) has been paid off, at which point repayments cease. With an income-related repayment, the borrowed amount can be regarded as a maximum value of repayment. Agents who are not very successful in the labor market repay less than received. Interestingly, most education economists seem to favor an income-related repayment. (Blaug, 1980, p. 45) has pointed out that "virtually every advocate of student loans in Britain [...] favors an income-related loans scheme [...] and not a personal loan repayable in a fixed number of years after taking up employment."

A graduate tax, however, is a tax supplement that applies only to graduates. If the graduate tax is regarded as a *repayment* for benefits received during the education period, the repayable amount may have the opposite effect to an income-related repayment of a loan. High-income graduates are pushed to *repay* more than they received. Graduates, in this case, are taxed twice. Glennerster (2003) and Glennerster et al. (2003) refer to two equity grounds that both date back to Adam Smith: capacity to pay and disproportionate benefit.

> As we argued [...] graduates disproportionately benefit from higher education in ways no other group does from investment made in them by their fellows. State funded lifetime expenditure on the higher education of the richest fifth is worth five times as much as that on the lowest fifth. A graduate tax combines the principles of ability to pay, disproportionate benefit and efficient collection. Adam Smith's perfect tax! (Glennerster, 2003, p. 26)

However, the concept of a graduate tax has been supported by several economists. Arrow (1993); Lincoln and Walker (1993) regard a graduate tax as a means to achieve a just contribution by students for the subsidies they received. Pennings (2000) pointed out that a graduate tax is an example for

[1] "Perhaps [...] the money which [the taxpayer] is required to pay directly out of his pocket is the only taxation which he is quite sure that he pays at all". (Mill, 1848[1994], p. 237).

a *zero expected cost* investment stimulus. García-Peñalosa and Wälde (2000) propose a lump-sum graduate tax in a model with capital-market imperfections and an uncertain outcome from the educational investment. The lump-sum graduate tax is higher than the received subsidy in order to finance the subsidies for those who also invest in higher education but do not pass a final exam. Finally, Poutvaara (2004) proposes a voluntary graduate tax and emphasizes that it can be seen as a triple dividend in new EU member states, "benefiting the emigrants, those left behind in the new member states and the old member states alike" (Poutvaara, 2004, p. 25).

One of the most popular advocates for an income-related loan is Nicholas Barr. He argue that the main advantage of an income-related loan with regard to *equity* is that "no-one repays more than he/she has borrowed" (Barr, 1989, p. 64). By arguing in this way, Barr unveils exactly the opposite view on equity compared to the view of Glennerster, referred to above.

The most obvious advantage of a graduate tax is that it would be relatively straightforward to introduce.[2] A graduate tax that is organized as a higher tax bracket in the income tax schedule can be raised without significant administrative costs. In particular, if the loan varies between agents (e.g. with respect to faculty, university, gender, and so on), it would be too complicated to recover the precise amount from each former student. The basic presumption is that administrative costs are minimized when a small scheme is *piggy-backed* onto a larger one like the income tax.

The differences between the two concepts discussed here, however, are not as great as they may appear initially. The main differences between a voluntary graduate tax and a loan scheme with income-related repayment can be seen when we consider that the outcome of education is uncertain. Assume, for example, that agents do not know exactly their innate endowment, although they are able to form an unbiased estimate of it. As in Levhari and Weiss (1974); Eaton and Rosen (1980), we assume that endowment is given by $x\,y_i$, where x is a random variable with a mean of unity and with support $[a_1 \geq 0, a_2]$. Note that agents are still risk-neutral. An agent with an expected endowment slightly above $\tilde{y}_0^{[p]}$ will also use the loan if its repayment is income-contingent. The repayment equals the loan if x, unveiled in the second period, is unity, while the agent will repay less than received if $x < 1$ but will not repay more otherwise. Agents with an endowment equal to $\tilde{y}_0^{[p]} + \varsigma$, where $\varsigma < a_1$, would also find it worthwhile to use the loan scheme as they have nothing to lose. The scheme, then, is a means not only to offset tax distortions, but also

[2] In this framework, we consider only a proportional tax system. Under this simple tax regime, the graduate tax is also simple to levy. However, under more complicated tax structures, in particular if taxation is progressive and, e.g. married couples can be taxed jointly, a graduate tax may create further problems. Consider, for example, if only one partner has invested in higher education. What should then be regarded as the tax base for the graduate tax? The author is indebted to Barbara Wolfe for highlighting this point.

to insure against uncertainty, which is not justified on efficiency grounds as agents are not risk-averse. Under a voluntary graduate tax, the agent with an endowment equal to $\tilde{y}_0^{[p]} + \varsigma$ would not demand the subsidy.

If a graduate tax is optional and the investment outcome is certain, the differences from a loan with income-related repayment vanish.

Nevertheless, a voluntary graduate tax is much more likely to achieve both goals, equity and efficiency, than the current practice in many European countries, as will be shown in the next section.

7.1 A Voluntary Graduate Tax

In the preceding section we emphasized that unwanted distributional consequences of public subsidization result primarily from the impracticability of discriminating between the subsidies granted to different students. The reason, as mentioned above, is the lack of information on individuals' endowments. This missing information is the main source of problematic equity effects.

In this subsection, we will demonstrate that a voluntary graduate tax could be used as a revelation mechanism. This funding scheme allows us both to support higher education up to an efficient level and to avoid the problematic distributional consequences better than unconditional grants, although it might be that both goals can only be approximately achieved simultaneously.

The model works as follows. Each agent is eligible for a subsidy to cover (partly) the direct costs of obtaining higher education, denoted by $\gamma \in [0,1] \subset \mathbb{R}$. Each agent can choose whether to obtain a subsidy in the first period and consequently to accept the graduate tax on his or her income as a graduate, or to opt out. In the latter case, second-period income is taxed by the constant tax rate $t \in [0,1) \subset \mathbb{R}$. Those who use the subsidy are additionally liable to a graduate tax on their income in the second period, denoted by β with $0 < \beta < (1-t)$, so that their second-period income is taxed by $t + \beta$.

As in the previous analysis, there are three groups. For the first group (group 1) it is still not worthwhile to invest in higher education. Group-2 agents will take out a subsidy and therefore complete a degree, while group-3 agents will invest in higher education without drawing on the funding system. The reason for the last group's decision is that the burden from the graduate tax exceeds the benefit from the loan. There exist, as a consequence, two educational-choice margins, an upper one and a lower one. The upper one denotes that agent who is indifferent about the alternatives, i.e. to draw on the funding scheme or not. However, for this agent it is worthwhile to invest in higher education in any case. Those agents with endowments below the lower educational-choice margin will, nevertheless, abstain from investing in higher education.

7.1.1 Optimal Policy

If we assume that the government's goal is efficiency, the government will set the rate of subsidization so that the lower educational-choice margin coincides with $\tilde{y}^{[bm]}$. For that, we need to consider a graduate's present value of net lifetime income after having drawn upon the scheme. It is given by

$$V_i^{E[1]} \equiv h\,y_i(1-t) - c(1-\gamma) + (1-t-\beta)y_i \cdot \frac{(1+u\,y_i)}{(1+r)} + \aleph. \tag{7.1}$$

The lower bound is then obtained by equating (7.1) and (6.4). It is given by

$$\begin{aligned}\tilde{y}^{[1]} \equiv & \frac{\psi\,(1-t)}{1-t-\beta} + \frac{\beta}{2u\,(1-t-\beta)} \\ & + \sqrt{\left[\frac{\psi\,(1-t)}{1-t-\beta} + \frac{\beta}{2u\,(1-t-\beta)}\right]^2 + \frac{\omega\,(1-\gamma)}{(1-t-\beta)}}.\end{aligned} \tag{7.2}$$

Proof. See Appendix G.3

The efficient educational-choice margin and $\tilde{y}^{[1]}$ coincide if the subsidy is set to

$$\gamma_1 \equiv t + \beta\left[1 + \tilde{y}^{[bm]}\theta\right] \tag{7.3}$$

where $\theta \equiv \frac{1}{c(1+r)} + \frac{(1-h)}{c}$.

Proof. See Appendix G.4.

It is obvious that the expression under the square root in (7.2) cannot become negative[3] for any value of γ less or equal to 1. Therefore, for every $0 \leq \gamma_1 \leq 1$ a solution that ensures efficiency exists. Furthermore, from the condition that $\gamma_1 \leq 1$ follows that the graduate tax cannot exceed $\hat{\beta}_1$, where

$$\hat{\beta}_1 \equiv \frac{1-t}{1+\theta\cdot\tilde{y}^{[bm]}}. \tag{7.4}$$

If γ is set equal to γ_1 to ensure efficiency, it is interesting to analyze the extent to which group-3 agents draw on the funding scheme. No one will do so if it is not advantageous for the least-talented agent in group 2 to draw on the subsidy in the first period. It is quite simple to derive a combination of γ and β, which ensures this goal: we equate a graduate's present value of lifetime income after having used the funding scheme, and the present value

[3] If the expression under the square root becomes negative, the economic intuition is the following: the higher γ the greater the size of agents with the lowest ability who invest in higher education. In this case (that we have ruled out), a fourth group of agents accrues starting from the left-hand side of the density function of y. If γ is so huge that the square root becomes negative, then no agent will reject an educational investment. See also Section 9.

of those graduates who renounced the scheme. Thus, we equate $V_i^{E[1]}$ which has already been derived in equation (7.1) and

$$V_i^{E[2]} \equiv hy_i(1-t) - c + (1-t)y_i \cdot \frac{(1+u\,y_i)}{(1+r)} + \aleph. \tag{7.5}$$

As the educational-choice margin we obtain[4]

$$\tilde{y}^{[2]} \equiv -\frac{1}{2u} + \sqrt{\frac{1}{4\,u^2} + \omega \cdot \frac{\gamma}{\beta}}. \tag{7.6}$$

Windfall gains are completely avoided if $\tilde{y}^{[2]} = \tilde{y}_0^{[p]}$. A subsidy that satisfies this condition is given by

$$\gamma_2 = \beta \left[\frac{1}{1-t} + \tilde{y}_0^{[p]} \cdot \theta \right]. \tag{7.7}$$

This upper bound divides those who invest in higher education into groups with and without use of the subsidy. For all $y_i > \tilde{y}^{[2]}$, it is worthwhile to opt out. Similarly to (7.4), the condition $0 \le \gamma_2 \le 1$ requires that the graduate-tax rate reaches its maximum value at

$$\hat{\beta}_2 \equiv \frac{1}{\frac{1}{(1-t)} + \theta \cdot \tilde{y}_0^{[p]}}. \tag{7.8}$$

7.1.2 Can Both Goals be Achieved Simultaneously?

In the preceding subsection we derived two values for γ, one that ensures efficiency (γ_1) and another that avoids windfall gains (γ_2). The government has to choose one of the two values, so it is not clear whether both goals can be achieved simultaneously. As both γ_1 and γ_2 depend on β, we can check for the possibility that a value of β exists that leads to $\gamma_1 = \gamma_2$. It is obvious that such a β-value exists, because γ_2 increases more strongly in β than γ_1 $\left(\frac{\partial\gamma_2}{\partial\beta} > \frac{\partial\gamma_1}{\partial\beta}\right)$,[5] but γ_1 intercepts the β-axis at t whereas γ_2 starts at the origin. On the other hand, to avoid windfall gains from the higher-education investment of agents with the lowest ability, we do not allow any γ to become greater than 1. As a consequence, it might be that a graduate tax that ensures coinciding values of γ_1 and γ_2 exceeds $\hat{\beta}_1$ or $\hat{\beta}_2$. Let us denote such a graduate-tax rate β that ensures coinciding values of γ_1 and γ_2 by β^*:

$$\beta^* = \frac{t(1-t)}{t + \theta(1-t)\left(\tilde{y}_0^{[p]} - \tilde{y}^{[bm]}\right)}. \tag{7.9}$$

Indeed, we can derive the following proposition:

[4] The same result can be obtained by equating $\gamma\, c$ and $\frac{\beta}{(1+r)}\, y_i\, (1+u\,y_i)$.

[5] This can be proved very easily: $\tilde{y}_0^{[p]} > \tilde{y}^{[bm]}$ and $\frac{1}{1-t} > t$.

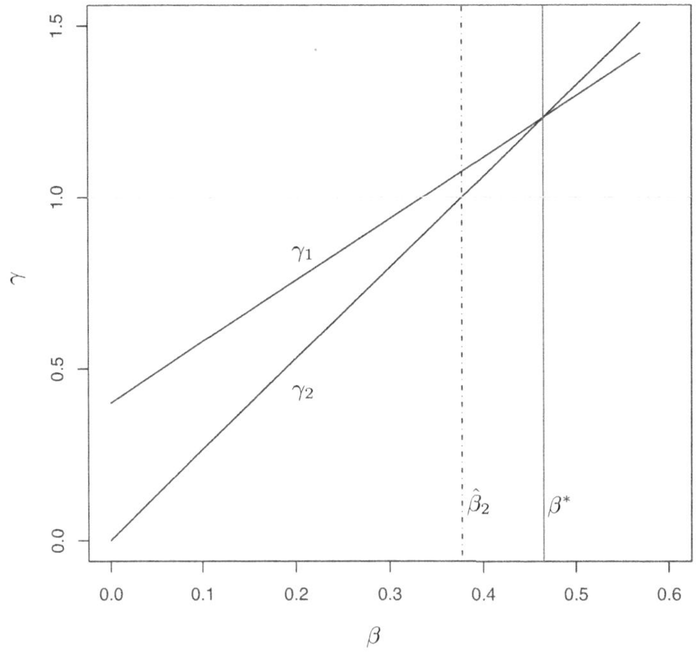

Fig. 7.1. $\gamma_1, \gamma_2, \hat{\beta}_2$ and β^*

Proposition 7.1. *It is not possible to achieve both goals simultaneously.*

Proof. To prove this, we show that $\beta^* > \hat{\beta}_2 \Leftrightarrow \frac{\beta^*}{\hat{\beta}_2} > 1$. This means that at the point of intersection between γ_1 and γ_2, both γ-values are greater than 1.[6] Considering (7.8) and (7.9), we obtain:

$$\frac{\beta^*}{\hat{\beta}_2} = \frac{t(1-t)\left[\frac{1}{(1-t)} + \theta \cdot \tilde{y}_0^{[p]}\right]}{t + \theta(1-t)\left[\tilde{y}_0^{[p]} - \tilde{y}^{[bm]}\right]}.$$

Division by $(1-t)$ yields

$$\frac{\beta^*}{\hat{\beta}_2} = \frac{t\left[\frac{1}{(1-t)} + \theta \tilde{y}_0^{[p]}\right]}{\frac{1}{(1-t)} + \theta\left[\tilde{y}_0^{[p]} - \tilde{y}^{[bm]}\right]}.$$

[6] Note that $\gamma_1'(\beta), \gamma_2'(\beta) > 0$ and $\gamma_1''(\beta) = \gamma_2''(\beta) = 0$. Thus, the point of intersection is unique.

The numerator can simplified to $\frac{t}{(1-t)} + t\theta\tilde{y}_0^{[p]}$, so that

$$\frac{\beta^*}{\hat{\beta}_2} = \frac{\frac{t}{(1-t)} + t\,\theta\tilde{y}_0^{[p]}}{\frac{t}{(1-t)} + \theta\tilde{y}_0^{[p]} - \theta\tilde{y}^{[bm]}}. \tag{7.10}$$

The numerator exceeds the denominator if $t \cdot \tilde{y}_0^{[p]} > \tilde{y}_0^{[p]} - \tilde{y}^{[bm]} \Leftrightarrow \tilde{y}^{[bm]} > (1-t)\tilde{y}_0^{[p]}$. To show this, we prove the following lemma:

Lemma 7.2. $\tilde{y}^{[bm]} > (1-t)\tilde{y}_0^{[p]}$.

Proof. The proof proceeds in three steps:

Step 1: $\tilde{y}^{[bm]} = \psi + \sqrt{\psi^2 + \omega}$. Confer (6.6).

Step 2: Eq. (6.7) multiplied by $(1-t)$ yields:$(1-t) \cdot \tilde{y}_0^{[p]} = (1-t)\,\psi + \sqrt{(1-t)^2\psi^2 + (1-t)\,\omega}$.

Step 3: As $t < 1$,

(a) $\psi > (1-t)\,\psi$,
(b) $\psi^2 > (1-t)^2\psi^2$,
(c) $\omega > (1-t)\,\omega$.

It follows from items (b) and (c) of step 3 that the square root in $\tilde{y}^{[bm]}$ is greater than the square root in $\tilde{y}_0^{[p]}$. From this and from (a) follows that $\tilde{y}^{[bm]} > (1-t)\tilde{y}^{[p]}$. □ □

Note that $\hat{\beta}_1 < \hat{\beta}_2$, so that β^* also exceeds $\hat{\beta}_1$. The idea behind this way to prove Proposition 7.1 is illustrated in Figure 7.1.

Given Proposition 7.1, the question that arises is: which combination of γ and β minimizes the windfall gains while maintaining efficiency? To answer this question we analyze the slope of $\tilde{y}^{[2]}(\gamma_1)$. It can be derived as follows: we insert γ_1 into $\tilde{y}^{[2]}$ and generate the first derivation with respect to β. By doing so we obtain

$$\frac{\partial\tilde{y}^{[2]}}{\partial\beta} = -\frac{t\,\omega}{2\,\beta^2 \cdot \sqrt{\left(-\frac{1}{2\,u}\right)^2 + \omega\,\frac{\gamma_1}{\beta}}}. \tag{7.11}$$

As ω, t, u, and β are positive, the slope is negative. The consequence of these properties is that the closer the graduate tax is to β^*, the smaller the number of agents who reap windfall gains. Thus, the higher γ_1, the closer $\tilde{y}^{[2]}$ is to $\tilde{y}_0^{[p]}$. The resulting curve is illustrated in Figure 7.2. The higher β, the closer this curve is to $\tilde{y}_0^{[p]}$. The gray horizontal lines represent the two educational-choice margins under consideration, the decreasing one represents $\tilde{y}^{[2]}(\gamma_1)$.

By considering the slope of $\tilde{y}^{[2]}(\gamma_1)$ and Proposition 7.1, we can derive the following Proposition:

Proposition 7.3. *If $\hat{\beta}_2 < \beta^*$, then the best policy is for the subsidy to cover the entire cost of obtaining higher education.*

Figure 7.2 illustrates the intuition for the Proposition 7.3.

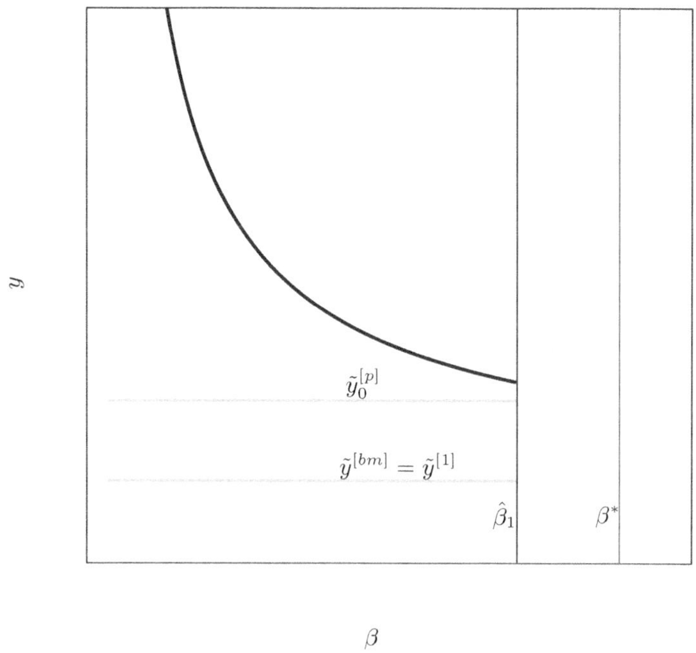

Fig. 7.2. Equity effects of an efficiency-orientated policy

Part III

The Role of Progressive Taxation

8

Offsetting Subsidies and Progressive Taxation

The following sections shed light on the distortive effect of various kinds of progressive taxation and infer the subsidy rate required to offset such distortions. The main purpose of the following analysis is threefold. First, under a pure proportional tax system the political implications of the argument in favor of subsidization is weak because it seems much more convenient to allow deductibility rather than to establish a large subsidization system. The following analysis, however, indicates that it does not suffice to allow for tax-deduction if we have to deal with income-tax progression. Second, in this chapter, we give a rationale or at least a normative justification for an interesting relationship which is plotted in Figures 8.1 and 8.2. In both figures, the Musgrave measure of progressivity[1] is plotted on the abscissae. The ordinate in Figure 8.1 shows the relative importance of higher-education subsidies relative to total public expenditure (data for 1990). Interestingly, the higher the progressivity, the higher is this relative value for almost all OECD countries. In Figure 8.2, some rates of subsidization are plotted. Unfortunately, due to a lack of data, only a few countries can be considered. Nevertheless, the plot provides evidence for a positive correlation between the rate of subsidization and the progressivity of income taxation. Third, we demonstrate that subsidies that offset existing tax distortions may be in league with the devil: by counteracting distortions, *new* inefficiencies may arise so that subsidies may fail to offset for tax distortions. By showing this, we moderate the optimistic view of subsidies found in some of the related literature, noted above. A consequence of our analysis is that international comparisons of education policy, as carried out e.g. by the (OECD, 2002, Ch. B), should not focus exclusively on the expenditure volume for educational institutions. Rather, they should take into account the comprehensive effect of public policy on human-capital formation, which clearly includes the tax system. Considering this, it seems

[1] The degree of progression is measured as "the ratio of the percentage change in income after tax to the percentage change in income before tax" (Musgrave and Thin, 1948, p. 507).

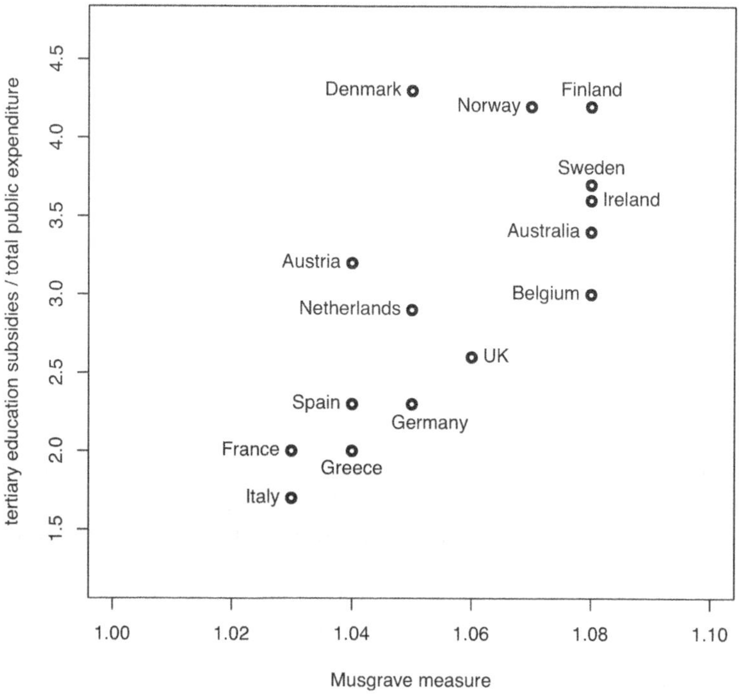

Fig. 8.1. Progressivity and Education Subsidies among OECD countries. Source: OECD (2002) and Norregaard (1990).

that differences among OECD countries are smaller than a first glance at subsidies might suggest.

Definition 8.1. *According to Pollak (1980), we define a proportional tax rate after a tax-free threshold as an indirectly progressive tax, and a tax schedule with increasing marginal tax rates as a directly progressive tax.*

Consider a complicated (comprehensive) income-tax schedule, which consists of a tax-free threshold and a higher marginal tax rate for high-income earners. Net lifetime earnings are equal to:

$$V_i^{E[d+ip]} = (1-t)h\,y_i - c(1-\rho) + t\,\kappa + \frac{(1+s_i)\,y_i(1-t-\varepsilon) + t\kappa}{1+r} + \aleph \quad (8.1)$$

and

$$V_i^{N[d+ip]} = y_i\,(1-t) + t\,\kappa + \frac{y_i\,(1-t) + t\kappa}{1+r} + \aleph. \quad (8.2)$$

Equating (8.1) and (8.2) and isolating y_i leads to the *ECM* of:

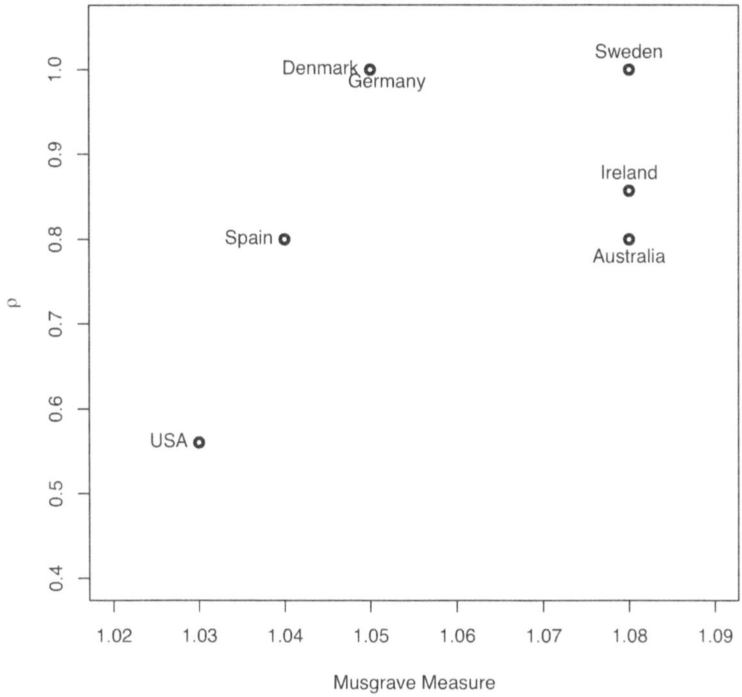

Fig. 8.2. Progressivity and ρ-Values for some OECD countries. Source: OECD (1993) and Norregaard (1990).

$$\tilde{y}^{[d+ip]} = -\frac{(1+r)(1-t)(h-1)-\varepsilon}{2\,u(1-t-\varepsilon)} + \sqrt{\left(-\frac{(1+r)(1-t)(h-1)-\varepsilon}{2\,u(1-t-\varepsilon)}\right)^2 + \frac{\omega(1-\rho)}{(1-t-\varepsilon}}. \tag{8.3}$$

The rate of subsidization that is required in order to compensate for the distorting impact of direct and indirect income-tax progression on $\tilde{y}$ can be found by equating (8.3) and (6.6). It is given by

$$\rho_1 \equiv t + \varepsilon\left[1 + \tilde{y}^{[bm]}\theta\right] \tag{8.4}$$

where, as before, $\theta \equiv \frac{1}{c(1+r)} + \frac{(1-h)}{c}$.

Proof. Substitute γ by ρ and β by ε in Appendix G.4. □

For the remainder of the discussion, it is useful to distinguish three special cases.

1. Indirect income-tax progression: $\kappa > 0$, $\varepsilon = 0$

2. Direct income-tax progression: $\kappa = 0$, $0 < \varepsilon < (1 - t)$
3. Indirect and direct income-tax progression: $\kappa > 0$, $0 < \varepsilon < (1 - t)$.

8.1 Indirect Income-Tax Progression

A lot of different groups of individuals would have to be considered under indirect income-tax progression: two groups of individuals who invest in higher education, and two groups that are below the *ECM*. One subgroup of those investing in human capital pays no taxes in the first period because the y_i of its members is below the threshold. Members of the second subgroup pay taxes in the first period as their basic income exceeds the threshold. Of those not investing in higher education, the first subgroup receives a basic income that is below the threshold. Hence, these individuals pay no taxes. The second group of individuals not investing in higher education pay taxes in both periods as their endowment exceeds the threshold ($y_i > \kappa$). Considering all these cases would certainly complicate the analysis. Therefore, it shall be assumed that the income of students during their qualification period does not exceed the threshold ($\kappa > h \cdot \hat{y}$) and that all non-graduates pay taxes in both periods.

The net lifetime earnings of non-graduates differ from those of graduates with earnings below the threshold only with regard to the double relief of the threshold (which, of course, has to be discounted in the second period). Introducing an indirect income-tax progression changes the net lifetime earnings of graduates in two ways. First, no income taxes are paid in the first period. Second, the threshold increases income in the second period by $\frac{t\kappa}{1+r}$.

In the second period, the relief due to the basic allowance is the same for both graduates and non-graduates. Therefore, the effect in the first period is crucial. In this case, the easing of $t\kappa$ for non-graduates is opposed by an easing of $h\,t\,y_i$ for graduates. As we have assumed above that the income of students during their qualification period does not exceed the threshold, $h\,y_i < \kappa$ applies. By comparing the relief accruing to graduate and non-graduates in the first period ($h\,t\,y_i$ versus $t\kappa$), it becomes clear that it is larger for the latter group. Therefore, it is expected that introducing a tax-free threshold will lead to a higher educational-choice margin than will proportional taxation.

With the restricting assumption made above, the net lifetime earnings of whose investing in higher education are

$$V_i^{E[ip]} = h\,y_i - c(1-\rho) + \frac{(1+s_i)\,y_i(1-t-\varepsilon) + t\kappa}{1+r} + \aleph \tag{8.5}$$

and that of non-educated are still given by eq. (8.2). The educational choice margin becomes more complicated, it is given by

$$\tilde{y}^{[ip]} = -\frac{(1+r)(h-1+t)-\varepsilon}{2\,u(1-t-\varepsilon)} + \sqrt{\left(-\frac{(1+r)(h-1+t)-\varepsilon}{2\,u(1-t-\varepsilon)}\right)^2 + \frac{\omega(1-\rho)}{(1-t-\varepsilon)} + \frac{t\,k(1+r)}{u(1-t-\varepsilon)}}. \tag{8.6}$$

Equating (8.6) and $\tilde{y}^{[bm]}$ yields the optimal rate of subsidization:

$$\rho = t\left[1 + \frac{\left(\kappa - h\,\tilde{y}^{[bm]}\right)}{c}\right]. \tag{8.7}$$

Proposition 8.2. *In the case of indirect income-tax progression, the distortion-correcting rate of subsidization has to be higher than the tax rate.*

Proof. First, the assumption that $\kappa > h \cdot \hat{y}$ implies $\kappa > h \cdot \tilde{y}^{[bm]}$. Second, c is strictly positive. □

Note that this and the other optimal subsidy rates yield only the necessary condition. As we will see in Chapter 9, optimality can be derived only if the rate of subsidization does not exceed unity.

8.2 Direct Income-Tax Progression

Application of increasing marginal tax rates to annual income discriminates against the taxpayer whose income fluctuates. If net lifetime earnings are identical, the direct income-tax progression results in an advantage for those individuals who can spread their net lifetime earnings evenly over a longer period of time. Thus, taxpayers with fluctuating incomes and taxpayers with steady incomes carry different burdens. Sturn and Wohlfahrt (2000) have recently labeled this additional burden *Foregone Smoothing Benefit*.

The present value of net lifetime earnings are given in eq. (8.1) and (8.2) where κ is set to zero. The same applies to the educational-choice margin in eq. (8.3). With the same procedure used in the preceding sections, we obtain the following optimal rate of subsidization:

$$\rho = t + \varepsilon\left(1 + y^{[bm]}\left[\frac{1}{c\,(1+r)} + \frac{(1-h)}{c}\right]\right). \tag{8.8}$$

Proposition 8.3. *The rate of subsidization has to exceed the tax rate to compensate for the distortionary impact of taxation on human-capital accumulation.*

Proof. This proposition is simple to prove because all values are nonnegative (whereas t, ε are strictly positive) and $h \leq 1$. □

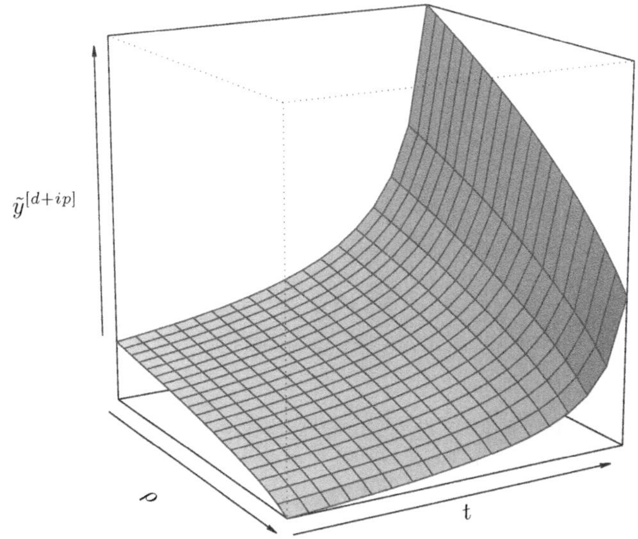

Fig. 8.3. *ECM* under a indirectly and directly progressive taxation

8.3 Direct and Indirect Income-Tax Progression

In the previous sections, we separated the effects for the most complicated case of a tax schedule with a tax-free threshold and an increasing marginal tax rate. This *combined* effect is illustrated in Figure 8.3. Summing up the previous sections, we can see that under this tax regime, the tax distortion is threefold. A distortion arises from the following sources:

- first, the nondeductibility of the direct costs of obtaining higher education. This was the sole distortion under the simple proportional tax regime;
- second, the fact that a tax-free threshold rewards those agents who do not invest in higher education, as long as we assume that students do not earn an amount above the threshold in the first period; and
- third, the application of the increasing tax rate to annual income, which discriminates against the taxpayer whose income fluctuates.

8.4 Concluding Remarks

In this chapter, we analyzed the combined effect of taxation and subsidization on human-capital formation. We supported the implications of recent literature that subsidies to higher education can enhance efficiency by offsetting existing distortions created by progressive taxation.

The implication of our analysis is that international comparisons of education policy, as carried out e.g. by the (OECD, 2002, Ch. B), should not focus exclusively on the expenditure volume for educational institutions. Rather, they should take into account the comprehensive effect of public policy on human-capital formation, which clearly includes the tax system. Considering this, it seems that differences among OECD countries are smaller than a first glance at subsidies might suggest.

9

Limits of Distortion-Offsetting Subsidies

As the preceding chapters have shown, the optimal rate of subsidization may be very high. If taxation is heavily distorting, it may be necessary for the subsidy rate to exceed unity in order to ensure an optimal educational-choice

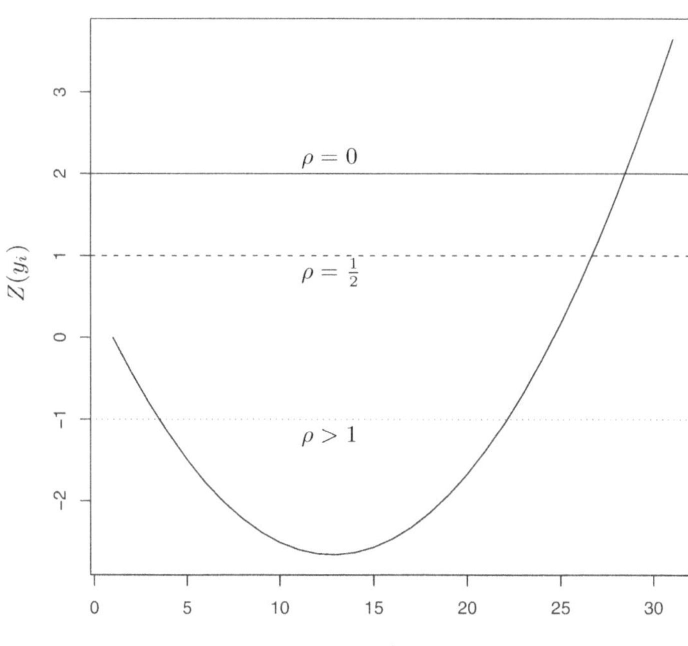

Fig. 9.1. The limiting effect of countervailing subsidies if they exceed unity

margin (in the second-best sense). However, if a subsidy rate greater than unity is required to reconstitute an educational-choice margin equal to $\tilde{y}^{[bm]}$, then subsidization fails to ensure optimality. The reason is that a subsidy rate greater than one means that the direct costs of obtaining higher education are totally borne by the state and each agent investing in higher education receives a grant. This grant may exceed the lifetime income of the less talented agents, thus encouraging them to invest in higher education, even though they are not suited to pursuing a degree. As a consequence, a fourth group of agents arises, starting from the left-hand side of the density function of y.

Thus, the higher the subsidy rate, the greater is the number of low-ability agents investing in higher education. This is illustrated in Figure 9.1. We denote by $Z(y_i)$, the surplus resulting from the increase in income due to educational investment less foregone earnings ($Z(y_i) = \frac{u\, y_i^2}{(1+r)} - (1-h)y_i$). Without subsidization and taxation, the educational-choice margin is given by the intersection of Z and c. Given $Z(0) = 0 < c$, the resulting educational-choice margin is unique. Next, we consider the case where half of the direct costs are subsidized, indicated by the dashed horizontal line. The educational-choice margin falls, but it is remains unique. The dotted line indicates the case where the subsidy rate exceeds unity (so that $(1-\rho)c$ becomes negative). In that case, a second educational-choice margin accrues according to the explanation already provided. If the $(1-\rho)c$-line bothers the minimum point of the Z-line, then nobody will abstain from investing in higher education.

This insight may provide a rationale for introducing ability tests when providing grants in order to correct distortions.

10

Summary and Conclusion

In recent decades, discussing the consequences of a given unwanted distributional impact of public higher education has become more and more important. Only to a lesser extent has there been focus on empirical investigations, the need for which has been ignored by both textbook authors and theorists.

Our analysis suggests that the question of distributional consequences is much more variegated than a glance at many textbooks and models would suggest. It is beyond controversy that a cross-sectional analysis is the most appropriate universe to deal with the impact on *rich* and *poor* households. Such studies have been carried out for many countries and the results indicate that the *Friedman-thesis* should be handled with some care. In contrast to a widespread belief among economists, the use of the net-transfer calculation provides an incidence, which is clearly in favor of the lower-income deciles. As noted above, the pattern of the net-transfer calculation depends to a great extent on the student representation effect. The student representation effect itself depends particularly on the general social stratification within and among the income deciles and on the selectivity of the educational system with respect to parents' incomes. Even if it is true that the processes of selection and allocation of students are more in favor of the upper-income brackets (in support of the thesis of many economists), the so-called level effect may overcompensate this structural effect.

However, cross-sectional distributional considerations are only part of the discussion. Most attention should be given to efficiency arguments. With regard to the normative justification for educational subsidization, this thesis has emphasized an efficiency justification for subsidies to higher education besides the classical arguments. We have shown that subsidizing education is optimal in a second-best sense, because it offsets the distortionary effects of taxation on human-capital accumulation.

Some authors argue that if an inefficiency can be counteracted by subsidies, the distributional effects on graduates and non-graduates may not be regressive because these groups can negotiate on the value-added. We have called this viewpoint into question by emphasizing the role of windfall gains, which are likely to vitiate this optimistic view. So far, this argument has been neglected in the related literature.

However, the thesis also shows that windfall gains are avoidable to a large extent. A voluntary graduate tax is shown to be a means of achieving this, and furthermore, as a self-selection mechanism. At least in our framework, a voluntary graduate tax offsets the distortionary role of taxation and is likely to be a means to establish a Pareto-superior policy to the mutual advantage of both graduates and non-graduates.

With regard to most countries, it is acceptable to assume that the median voter is not a graduate. From the viewpoint of political economy, one might ask how it is possible that the median voter accepts a public funding towards a minority of individuals (see Harms and Zink (2003) for an overview). But such a question confuses the political economy that predominated at the time of the introduction of the unconditional funding system in its historical context with the political economy of public higher education under the present circumstances. Our analysis indicates that an equity-efficiency trade-off does not necessarily apply if the graduation rate is very low, because the pure windfall profits are quite small under these circumstances.

Many European countries have found themselves in similar situations in the years following World War II. A good example for the political economy during the 60s is provided by German history. The demographic consequences of World War II led to a lack of schoolteachers and to an increasing number of pupils. Forecasts indicated a dramatic situation in the schools due to a lack of students who were about to become a teacher. Indeed, the education minister of the region North-Rhine/Westphalia, Mikaz, asked housewives (so-called *Mikätzchen*) to teach pupils in the elementary school system in order to soften the lack of teachers.

Figure 10.1 demonstrates the development of the graduation rates in Germany over the last four decades. In 1960, roughly 6% of a cohort invested in higher education. Several measures of packages led to an increase of the rate in the 60s and 70s, but the huge increase took place in the 80s.

Most public attention provoked Picht's proclamation of the *Bildungskatastrophe* (education disaster) (see Picht (1964)) and the so-called Sputnik-shock. Public opinion was clearly in favor of public funding, which was viewed as an instrument to encourage investments in human capital. In this historical context, the extensive system of public funding has been established which is, as noted above, also explainable from a political-economics perspective.

Another question concerns the current circumstances. Most historians confirm that the problems of the 60s have been solved with a broad subsidization policy. But the persistence of a system which experienced only few incremental reforms in the last decades seems to be an anachronism today. The main problems of the 60s have been *more than solved* which is indicated by the large number of students who wish to become a teacher but cannot find employment. With regard to this development, it is not astonishing that the pendulum seems to have swung in favor of reduced fiscal activities in the

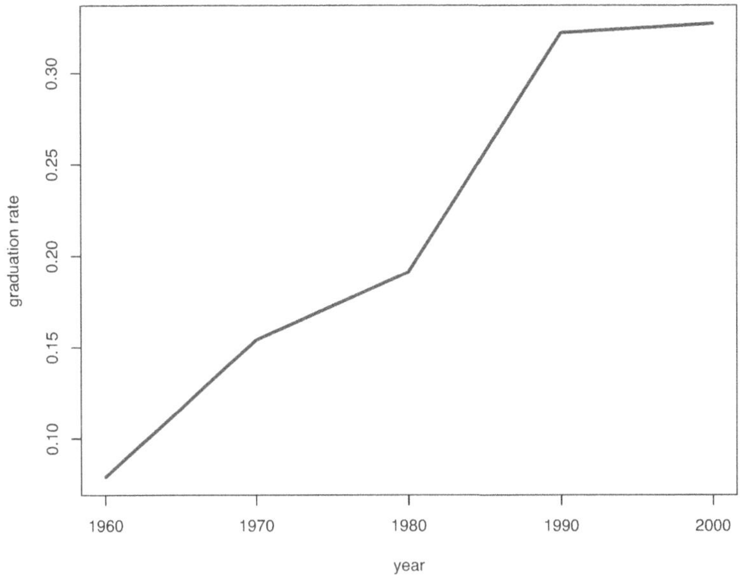

Fig. 10.1. Graduation rates in Germany over the last 40 years. Source: (bmbf, 2002, p. 152) and (bmbf, 1999a, p. 140)

higher-education sector. Some polls (see e.g. Centrum für Hochschulentwicklung (2003)) and the program of some political parties might be seen as an expression of the changed public opinion.

Part IV

Appendix

A

Appendix to the GSOEP

The German Socio-Economic Panel (GSOEP) is a longitudinal household survey conducted on an annual basis since 1984. In the first wave, some 12,000 individuals aged 16 and over, and distributed across roughly 6,000 households, were interviewed. The information available is drawn from the statements of the individuals. Due to panel attrition, sample size reduces somewhat each year, but in 1998, a refreshment sample of about 2,000 persons was added to the data base and in 2000, another sample of about 11,000 new individuals was included. Initially, the sample only referred to residents in West Germany, but following German unification, the sample was extended to the former German Democratic Republic in 1990. The GSOEP is representative of the population residing in Germany and contains a large number of socioeconomic variables on demography, education, employment, income, housing, health, and so forth. For further information on the GSOEP, see Haisken-DeNew and Frick (2000).

B

A Brief Glance on Bootstrap Confidence Intervals

"This is not an argument against
theory, of course, only
against unnecessary theory"
(Efron and Tibshirani, 1986, p. 55).

B.1 The Basic Idea and Application to Public Economics

A basic reason why economics students and those from most other disciplines have to deal with statistics at the beginning of their study is that most scientific disciplines deal with samples rather than with population. As a consequence, almost all empirical work has to consider the problem of accuracy. An introductory example in most textbooks is the accuracy of a sample mean whereas the most common way of indicating statistical accuracy is the use of *standard errors*. Suppose that x is a real-valued random variable with probability distribution F. The standard error of the mean $\bar{x}$, written $\hat{\sigma}$, is the square root of the variance of $\bar{x}$. Roughly speaking, we expect $\bar{x}$ to be less than one standard error away from the expectation of F about 68% of the time, and less than two standard errors away about 95% of the time.

In most cases there is no equivalent to the $\hat{\sigma}$, which expresses the standard error as a simple function of the sampling distribution. As a consequence, formulas for the standard error do not exist for most statistics which are commonly used in public economics and possibly also in other disciplines. This lack is probably the reason for the missing attempt to determine statistical inference in many studies. The large amount of literature on income inequality is a good example and another is the whole literature on the distributional effect of public higher education, as mentioned in Part I.

An advisable method for generating confidence intervals is to bootstrap. The bootstrap is a general methodology for answering questions concerning the accuracy of an estimator. It is a computer-based method, which substitutes considerable amounts of computation in place of theoretical analysis.

We will present two closely-related methods of using the bootstrap to set confidence intervals. We have discussed obtaining $\hat{\sigma}$ of a particular estimator, let us denote it as θ. We will see that bootstrap confidence intervals can automatically incorporate often-used procedures to improve the normal approximation like the $tanh^{-1}$-transformation. The basic algorithm for estimating standard errors can simply be constructed in three steps, as has been expressed in (Efron and Tibshirani, 1993, Figure 6.1).

1. Select B independent bootstrap samples $\mathbf{x}^{*1}, \mathbf{x}^{*2}, \ldots, \mathbf{x}^{*B}$, each consisting of n data values drawn with replacement from $\mathbf{x}$, where $\mathbf{x}$ denotes the *real* sample.
2. Evaluate the bootstrap replication corresponding to each bootstrap sample,
$$\hat{\theta}^*(b) = s\left(\mathbf{x}^{*b}\right) \qquad b = 1, 2, \ldots, B.$$
where $s(\cdot)$ denotes a function (e.g. the function for an inequality measure).
3. Estimate the standard error by the sample standard deviation of the B replications
$$\hat{\sigma}_B = \sqrt{\frac{\sum_{b=1}^{B}[\hat{\theta}^*(b) - \hat{\theta}^*(\cdot)]^2}{(B-1)}}$$
where $\hat{\theta}^*(\cdot) \equiv \frac{\sum_{b=1}^{B}\hat{\theta}^*(b)}{B}$.

B.2 Percentile Method

The simplest way to compute a confidence interval is the use of the percentile method. Analogously to the three steps, it generates for each bootstrap sample a bootstrap estimator. For instance, we wish to obtain the confidence interval for a Gini coefficient. From the sample we have generated an estimator of the real coefficient. Now, compute for each bootstrap sample a new Gini coefficient so that we generate B coefficients. Then, we sort these generated coefficients in ascending order and the $B \cdot \alpha$ coefficient gives the lower bound of the confidence interval with 95 % confidence and $B \cdot (1-\alpha)$ the upper bound. More generally, let $\hat{G}$ be the cumulative distribution function of the bootstrap estimators $\hat{\theta}^*$. The $1-2\alpha$ percentile interval is defined by the α and $(1-\alpha)$ percentiles of $\hat{G}$. Hence, we can write the percentile interval as

$$\left[\hat{\theta}_{lb}, \hat{\theta}_{ub}\right] = \left[\hat{\theta}^{*(\alpha)}, \hat{\theta}^{*(1-\alpha)}\right].$$

For further discussion on the percentile method, in particular with respect to the range-preserving property, the transformation-respecting property and the coverage performance, see the detailed descriptions in (Efron and Tibshirani, 1993, Ch. 13).

Unfortunately, the use of the percentile method can lead to serious problems if, for example, the estimator might be a biased normal estimate,

$$\hat{\theta} \sim N(\theta + \texttt{bias}, \hat{\sigma}^2)$$

in which case no transformation can fix up the problem which arises from the existence of the bias.

B.3 BC_a Method

Problems like this one can be solved by using a more tedious bootstrap method, called *bias-corrected and accelerated* bootstrap, BC_a. Efron recommends the use of this kind of bootstrap method in particular for non-parametric purposes. However, the understanding of the percentile method is crucial for the understanding of the BC_a method.

The BC_a interval bounds are also given by percentiles of the bootstrap distribution, but are not necessarily the same ones. We will immediately see under which circumstances the BC_a bounds are the same as those obtained by the percentile method. The percentiles used by the BC_a method depend on two numbers, $\hat{a}$ (acceleration, denoted by acc) and $\hat{z}_0$ (bias-correction). The BC_a interval of intended coverage $1 - 2\alpha$, is given by $(\hat{\theta}_{lb}, \hat{\theta}_{ub}) = (\hat{\theta}^{*(\alpha_1)}, \hat{\theta}^{*(\alpha_2)})$, where

$$\alpha_1 = \Phi\left(\hat{z}_0 + \frac{\hat{z}_0 + z^{(\alpha)}}{1 - \mathsf{acc}(\hat{z}_0 + z^{(\alpha)})}\right) \quad \text{and}$$

$$\alpha_2 = \Phi\left(\hat{z}_0 + \frac{\hat{z}_0 + z^{(1-\alpha)}}{1 - \mathsf{acc}(\hat{z}_0 + z^{(1-\alpha)})}\right).$$

$\Phi(\cdot)$ denotes the standard normal cumulative distribution function and $z^{(\alpha)}$ is the $100\alpha^{th}$ percentile point of a standard normal distribution.

If $\hat{a}, \hat{z}_0 = 0$, then obviously $\alpha_1 = \Phi(z^{\alpha}) = \alpha$ and $\alpha_2 = \Phi\left(z^{1-\alpha}\right) = 1 - \alpha$ and any difference between the percentile and the BC_a method vanishes. The intuition becomes clear if one considers the nature of the bias-correction. It measures the median bias of $\hat{\theta}^*$. This means that if half of the $\hat{\theta}^*(b)$ values are less than or equal to $\hat{\theta}$, then the bias-correction is zero. The value of z_0 is obtained directly from the number of bootstrap replications less than the original estimate $\hat{\theta}$, relative to the total number of bootstrap replications, B,

$$\hat{z}_0 = \Phi^{-1}\left(\frac{1}{B} \cdot \left[\#\{\hat{\theta}^*(b) < \hat{\theta}\}\right]\right)$$

where Φ^{-1} indicating the inverse function of a standard normal cdf.

There exist several ways to generate the acceleration value, $\hat{a}$. A very tedious one is provided by (DiCiccio and Efron, 1996, section 3) whereas a simpler one is provided by (Efron and Tibshirani, 1993, Ch. 14).

Put together both, the acceleration and the bias-correction, the find the BC_a endpoints by

$$\hat{\theta}_{BC_a}[\alpha] = \hat{G}^{-1}\Phi\left(z_0 + \frac{z_0 + z^{(\alpha)}}{1 - a\left(z_0 + z^{(\alpha)}\right)}\right).$$

B.4 Conclusion

The bootstrap has become a well-known way to deal with statistical purposes in a wide range of applications. However, (Davison and Hinkley, 1997, Ch. 2.6.4) highlight three cases in which the bootstrap might fail:

1. Incomplete Data
2. Dependent data and
3. Dirty data.

Although true, problems like these may also cause failures by using some *traditional* methods of statistical inference. For instance, if a sample of income data contains only households being part of the top decile, each statistical method will produce bad results.

The main question, however, is not whether the bootstrap is the best of all thinkable and available methods, but whether to make attempt to statistical inference or not. As has been put forth, many studies, in particular those related to public economics, neglect this need, even if the resulting lack is obvious.

B.5 Bootstrapping in `R`

As noted above, bootstrap is a computer-intensive method. Hence, hardware as well as appropriate software is required. Efron and Tibshirani (1993) provide several applications for the statistical software S-Plus and `R`. `R` can be regarded as an implementation of the S language which was developed at Bell Laboratories. The S language forms the basis of the S-Plus systems. S-Plus is a commercial software. `R`, on the other hand, is a statistical software, made available under the General Public License (GPL). This means that the source code is freely available. It is often said that `R` is free software. The term "free" refers to ones freedom to run, copy, distribute, study, change and improve the software. `R` is part of the GNU Project. It was launched more than 20 years ago to develop a complete and freely available operating system.

In particular, the `R`-package `bootstrap` contains (almost) all functions and data sets from Efron and Tibshirani (1993). The most important functions, examples, and data sets from Davison and Hinkley (1997) are also available in a `R`-package called `boot`. All BC_a calculations in this book have been done by using the `bcanon` function in the `bootstrap` package. Measures of inequality are provided by the package `ineq`.

For more information, please confer R Development Core Team (2004); Venables et al. (2001); Dalgaard (2002). The home page for `R`, http://www.R-project.org, provides access to a panoply of resources and information, including a link to the Comprehensive R Archive Network (CRAN), from which R software can be downloaded for a variety of Unix and Linux platforms, for the Apple macintosh, and also for Microsoft products. The xtable package provides a helpful interaction with LaTeX.

C

Summary Statistics for the HIS Data

Figure C.1 illustrates the distribution of the household size (number of household members) among the households listed in the HIS-data set. The effect of this distribution on the difference between the distribution of monthly unweighted net income and weighted net income (using the square-root scale) is depicted in Figure C.2. It contains two box plots. A box plot, also known as a box and whisker diagram, provides an excellent visual summary of many important aspects of a distribution. The box stretches from the first quartile to the third quartile. The median is shown as a line across the box. Therefore a quarter of the distribution is between this line and the top of the box and a quarter of the distribution is between this line and the bottom of the box.

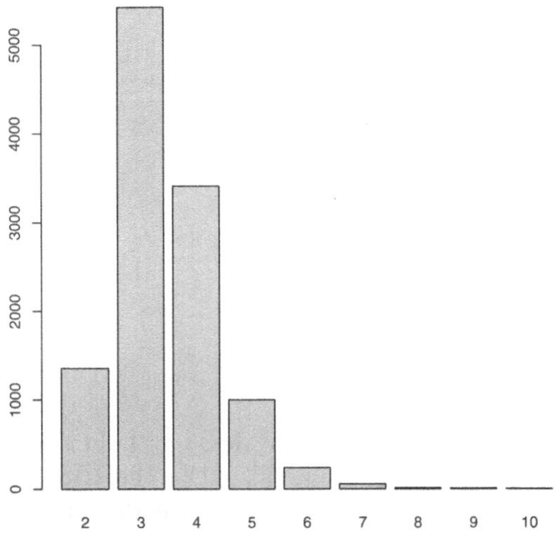

Fig. C.1. Distribution of the household size

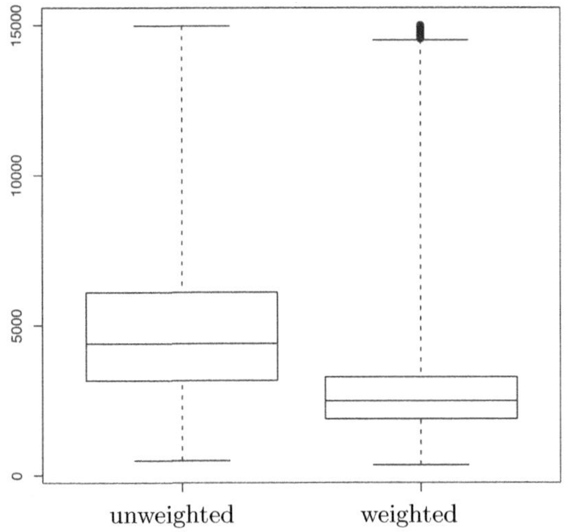

Fig. C.2. Unweighted and weighted net incomes compared

D

Summary Statistics for the GSOEP Data

Figure D.1 depicts the distribution of the four income concepts used in Part 1 for West Germany in 1997. The distribution of the household size and the number of children living in a household in West Germany in 1997 are depicted in Figure D.2. Source: GSOEP

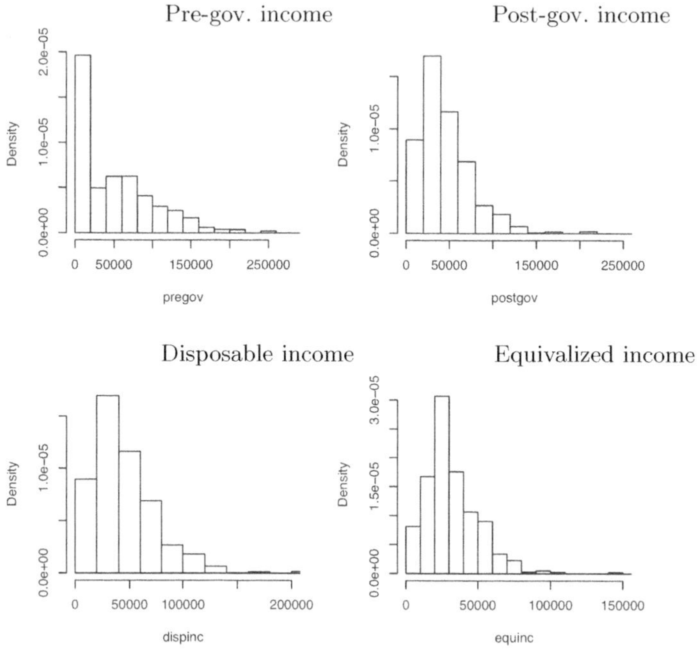

Fig. D.1. Pre-gov. income, post-gov. income, disposable income and equivalized income

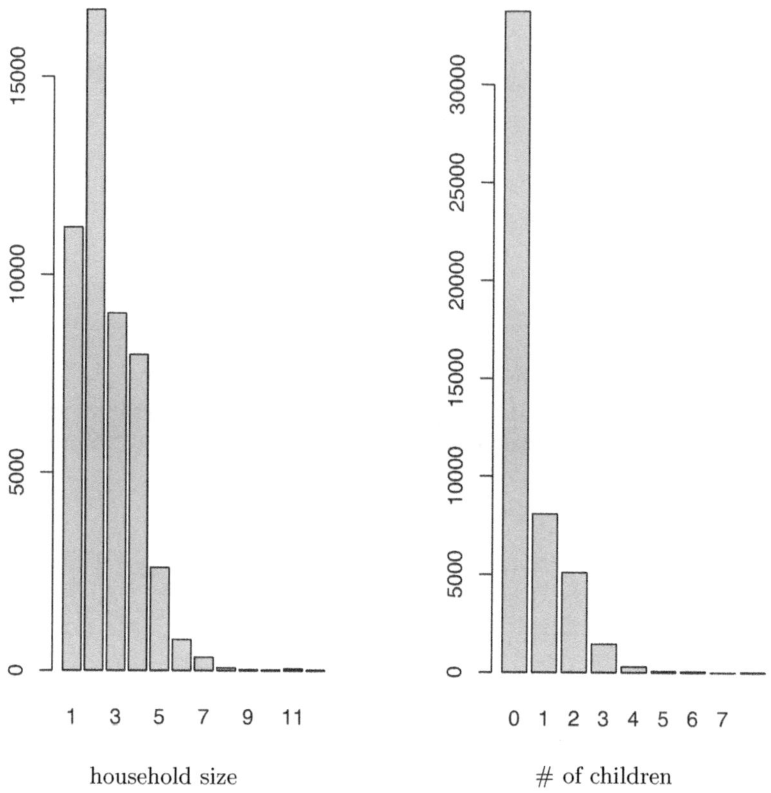

Fig. D.2. Household size and number of children in German households 1997

E

Educational-Choice Margins Under Progressive Taxation

In addition to Figure 8.3, we provide two additional plots for the educational-choice margin for various $t-$ and ρ-values under indirect and direct income-tax progression.

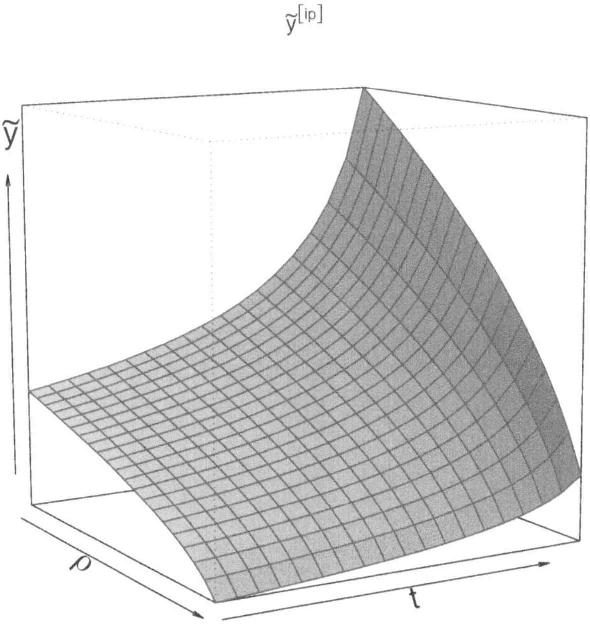

Fig. E.1. Educational-choice margin: indirect income-tax progression

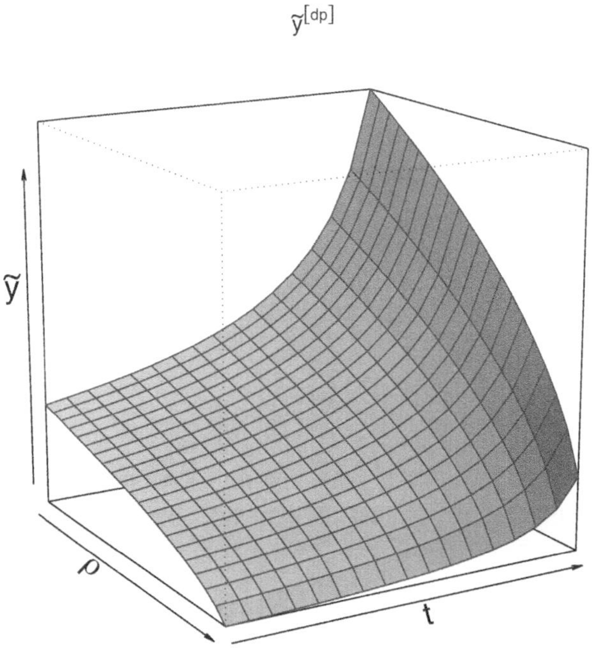

Fig. E.2. Educational-choice margin: direct income-tax progression

F

The Benefit and Cost Function Under a Directly and Indirectly Progressive Income-Tax System

The cost function in that case is larger than indicated in equation (6.10) because earnings of students in the first period are not taxed due to the tax-free threshold. The foregone tax revenue is therefore the entire taxes paid by those who would not take up a degree without subsidization. Let us denote the (per capita) cost function under a complicated tax regime as C^*, then we can rework (6.10) to

$$C^* \equiv p(\rho) \cdot \rho c + t \int_{\tilde{y}_{(\rho=0)}}^{\tilde{y}_{(\rho>0)}} y \, dF(y). \tag{F.1}$$

The (per capita) benefit function under a direct and indirect income tax pro-

	ρ	W	$\aleph$	p
	0.00	96.82	0.048	0.17
	0.20	99.47	0.049	0.22
	0.40	101.35	0.048	0.27
	0.60	102.62	0.047	0.37
$\rho^* \approx$	0.63	102.64	0.046	0.38
	0.80	100.90	0.040	0.54
	1.00	91.27	0.024	0.83

Table F.1. Numerical example for a directly progressive taxation.

gression looks much more different from (6.11). The reason is as follows: the additional tax revenue under a proportional tax regime is equal to t multiplied by the earnings which arise from the private rentability of higher education (see (6.11)). This earning part is now taxed by $t + \varepsilon$ instead of t alone. Furthermore, the second period earnings are taxed by ε, so that the (6.11) can be reworked to

$$B^* \equiv \frac{(t+\varepsilon)u \int\limits_{\tilde{y}(\rho=0)}^{\tilde{y}(\rho>0)} y^2\, dF(y) + \varepsilon \int\limits_{\tilde{y}(\rho=0)}^{\tilde{y}(\rho>0)} y\, dF(y)}{(1+r)}. \tag{F.2}$$

It is not necessary to subtract the costs from the benefits as it has been done above. The main and most important insights can be obtained if we compare (F.1) with (6.10) and (F.2) with (6.11), respectively.

A tax regime which consists of a tax-free threshold creates more foregone tax revenues and a direct tax progression leads to higher tax revenues. The foregone revenue created by the threshold amounts to

$$h \cdot t \int\limits_{\tilde{y}(\rho=0)}^{\tilde{y}(\rho>0)} y\, dF(y)$$

and the extended revenue due to increasing marginal tax rates amounts to

$$\frac{\varepsilon \cdot u \int\limits_{\tilde{y}(\rho=0)}^{\tilde{y}(\rho>0)} y^2\, dF(y) + \varepsilon \int\limits_{\tilde{y}(\rho=0)}^{\tilde{y}(\rho>0)} y\, dF(y)}{(1+r)}.$$

Note that the upper bound of the integrals in (F.1) and (F.2) may have different values as those in (6.10) and (6.11).

The equity and efficiency effects of a subsidization which countervails the distortion of a direct tax progression is shown in table F.1. In this numerical example, the optimal rate of subsidization is approximately 0.633. The closer ρ to ρ^*, the higher W, which denotes the utilitarian welfare. Due to the windfall gains, however, the lump-sum transfer declines. The higher ρ, the higher the graduation rate.

G

Some Proofs and Derivatives

G.1 The Educational-Choice Margin Under Proportional Taxation

The present values of the net lifetime income of educated agents, V^E, and of non-educated ones, V^N, were given by . (6.3) and (6.4):

$$V_i^E = (1-t)h\, y_i - c(1-\rho) + \frac{(1-t)\, y_i\, (1+u\, y_i)}{1+r} + \aleph,$$

$$V_i^N = (1-t)\, y_i + \frac{(1-t)\, y_i}{1+r} + \aleph.$$

Equation both yields:

$$(1-t)y_i(h-1) + y^2\frac{u(1-t)}{(1+r)} - c(1-\rho) = 0$$

$$\Leftrightarrow$$

$$y^2 + y\frac{(1-t)(h-1)(1+r)}{u(1-t)} - c\frac{(1-\rho)(1+r)}{u(1-t)}.$$

Let $\psi \equiv \frac{(1-h)(1+r)}{2u}$ and $\omega \equiv \frac{c}{u}\,(1+r)$, then

$$\tilde{y}_{1,2}^{[p]} \equiv \psi \pm \sqrt{\psi^2 + \omega \cdot \frac{(1-\rho)}{(1-t)}}. \tag{G.1}$$

As ω, ρ, and t are all nonnegative, and $\rho \in [0,1]$, $t \in [0,1)$, $\tilde{y}_2^{[p]}$ is negative because the square root exceeds ψ. Hence, $\tilde{y}_1^{[p]}$ is unique in the relevant range.

G.2 Educational-Choice Margin: Benchmark Case

We labelled the non-interventionist, redistribution-free equilibrium, where the government does not implement any income policy, so that the educational-choice margin is fully determined by market forces. This benchmark case is determined by $\rho = t = 0$. The educational-choice margin in this benchmark case can be derived by setting $\rho = t = 0$ in eq. (G.1). It yields:

$$\tilde{y}^{[bm]} = \psi + \sqrt{\psi^2 + \omega}. \tag{G.2}$$

The optimal rate of subsidization, ρ^* can be derived by setting (G.1) = (G.2):

$$\begin{aligned}
& \sqrt{\psi^2 + \omega \cdot \frac{(1-\rho)}{(1-t)}} = \sqrt{\psi^2 + \omega} \quad | \uparrow^2 \\
\Leftrightarrow \quad & \psi^2 + \omega \frac{(1-\rho)}{(1-t)} = \psi^2 + \omega \quad | - \psi \\
\Leftrightarrow \quad & \omega \cdot \frac{(1-\rho)}{(1-t)} = \omega \quad | : \omega \\
\Leftrightarrow \quad & (1-\rho) = (1-t) \\
\Leftrightarrow \quad & \rho = t.
\end{aligned}$$

G.3 The Lower Educational-Choice Margin

The lower educational-choice margin (7.2) in a system with proportional taxation and a voluntary graduate-tax scheme is obtained by equating a graduate's present value of net lifetime income after having drawn upon the scheme and the present value of net lifetime income without graduation. Thus, we equate (7.1) and (6.4).

Consider first that the present value of second-period income of a graduate who is liable to a graduate tax, $(1 - t - \beta) y_i \cdot \frac{(1+u\, y_i)}{(1+r)}$, simplifies to

$$y_i \frac{1-t}{1+r} + y_i^2 \frac{u(1-t-\beta)}{(1+r)} - y_i \frac{\beta}{(1+r)}$$

so that the fist term equals second-period income of a non-graduate. Thus, equating (7.1) and (6.4) reads

$$\begin{aligned}
& y_i\,(1-t)(h-1) - c(1-\gamma) \frac{u(1-t-\beta)}{(1+r)} y_i^2 - y_i \frac{\beta}{(1+r)} = 0 \\
& y_i \frac{(1-t)(h-1)(1+r) - \beta}{(1+r)} + -c(1-\gamma) \frac{u(1-t-\beta)}{(1+r)} y_i^2 = 0 \\
& y_i^2 + y_i \cdot \frac{(1-t)(h-1)(1+r) - \beta}{u(1-t-\beta)} - \frac{c(1-\gamma)(1+r)}{u(1-t-\beta)} = 0,
\end{aligned}$$

Isolating y_i yields

$$\tilde{y}_{1,2} = -\frac{(1-t)(h-1)(1+r)-\beta}{2\,u(1-t-\beta)} \pm\sqrt{\left[-\frac{(1-t)(h-1)(1+r)-\beta}{2\,u(1-t-\beta)}\right]^2+\frac{c(1-\gamma)(1+r)}{u(1-t-\beta)}}. \tag{G.3}$$

Inserting ψ and ω, this expression simplifies to

$$\tilde{y}_{1,2} \equiv \frac{\psi\,(1-t)}{1-t-\beta}+\frac{\beta}{2u\,(1-t-\beta)} \pm\sqrt{\left[\frac{\psi\,(1-t)}{1-t-\beta}+\frac{\beta}{2u\,(1-t-\beta)}\right]^2+\frac{\omega\,(1-\gamma)}{(1-t-\beta)}}. \tag{G.4}$$

As $\omega > 0, y \in [0,1], \beta \in [0,(1-t)[$, the square root exceeds the first term so that $\tilde{y}_2 \leq 0$. As $y \in \mathbb{R}_{++}$ by assumption, $\tilde{y}_1 \equiv \tilde{y}^{[1]}$ is the unique solution.

G.4 The Optimal Subsidy Rate cum Voluntary Graduate Tax

Eq. (7.3) yields the subsidy rate which ensures efficiency under a subsidy cum voluntary graduate tax system. It is given by

$$\gamma_1 \equiv t+\beta\left[1+\tilde{y}^{[bm]}\theta\right]$$

where $\theta \equiv \frac{1}{c(1+r)}+\frac{(1-h)}{c}$. To derive (7.3), the educational-choice margin in the benchmark-case and lower educational-choice margin in a system with proportional taxation and a voluntary graduate-tax scheme (7.2) are equated. This can be proved as follows:

Let

$$a \equiv \frac{\psi\,(1-t)}{1-t-\beta}+\frac{\beta}{2u\,(1-t-\beta)} = \frac{(1-h)(1+r)(1-t)+\beta}{2\,u(1-t-\beta)},$$

then

$$\frac{\psi\,(1-t)}{1-t-\beta}+\frac{\beta}{2u\,(1-t-\beta)} +\sqrt{\left[\frac{\psi\,(1-t)}{1-t-\beta}+\frac{\beta}{2u\,(1-t-\beta)}\right]^2+\frac{\omega\,(1-\gamma)}{(1-t-\beta)}} = \tilde{y}^{[bm]}$$

simplifies to

$$a+\sqrt{a^2+\frac{\omega\,(1-\gamma)}{(1-t-\beta)}} = \tilde{y}^{[bm]}.$$

Thus,

$$\tilde{y}^{[bm]} - a = \sqrt{a^2 + \frac{\omega\,(1-\gamma)}{(1-t-\beta)}} \quad | \uparrow^2$$

$\Leftrightarrow$

$$\left(\tilde{y}^{[bm]}\right)^2 - 2\,a\,\tilde{y}^{[bm]} + a^2 = a^2 + \frac{\omega(1-\gamma)}{(1-t-\beta)}$$

$\Leftrightarrow$

$$\left(\tilde{y}^{[bm]}\right)^2 - 2\,a\,\tilde{y}^{[bm]} = \frac{\omega(1-\gamma)}{(1-t-\beta)}$$

$\Leftrightarrow$

$$\frac{\left(\tilde{y}^{[bm]}\right)^2 (1-t-\beta)}{\omega} - \frac{2\,a\,(1-t-\beta)\,\tilde{y}^{[bm]}}{\omega} = (1-\gamma) \tag{G.5}$$

Lemma G.1.

$$\frac{\left(\tilde{y}^{[bm]}\right)^2}{\omega} = 1 + \frac{(1-h)\tilde{y}^{[bm]}}{c} \tag{G.6}$$

Proof. $\omega \equiv \frac{c\,(1+r)}{u}$ by definition and $\tilde{y}^{[bm]}$ can be rearranged to

$$\frac{(1+r)}{2\,u}\left[(1-h) + \sqrt{(1-h)^2 + \frac{4c\,u}{(1+r)}}\right].$$

Thus,

$$\begin{aligned}
&\frac{\left(\tilde{y}^{[bm]}\right)^2}{\omega} = \\
&= \frac{(1+r)}{4\,c\,u}\left(2(1-h)^2 + 2(1-h)\sqrt{(1-h)^2 + \frac{4c\,u}{(1+r)}} + \frac{4c\,u}{(1+r)}\right) \\
&= \frac{(1+r)(1-h)^2}{2c\,u} + \frac{(1+r)(1-h)}{2c\,u}\sqrt{(1-h)^2 + \frac{4c\,u}{(1+r)}} + 1 \\
&= 1 + \frac{(1+r)(1-h)}{2c\,u}\left[(1-h) + \sqrt{(1-h)^2 + \frac{4c\,u}{(1+r)}}\right] \\
&= 1 + \frac{(1-h)}{c}\cdot\underbrace{\frac{(1+r)}{2\,u}\left[(1-h) + \sqrt{(1-h)^2 + \frac{4c\,u}{(1+r)}}\right]}_{\tilde{y}^{[bm]}}
\end{aligned}$$

□

With Lemma G.1, eq. (G.5) simplifies to

$$1-\gamma = (1-t-\beta)\left[1+\frac{(1-h)\tilde{y}^{[bm]}}{c} - \frac{2\,a}{\omega}\tilde{y}^{[bm]}\right]$$
$$= 1-t-\beta+\tilde{y}^{[bm]}\frac{(1-t-\beta)(1-h)}{c}$$
$$-\left[\tilde{y}^{[bm]}\frac{(1-h)(1-t)}{c}+\frac{\beta\tilde{y}^{[bm]}}{c(1+r)}\right]$$

Isolating γ yields

$$\gamma = t+\beta+\tilde{y}^{[bm]}\left[\frac{\beta(1-h)}{c}+\frac{\beta}{c(1+r)}\right]$$

and therefore

$$\gamma = t+\beta\left[1+\tilde{y}^{[bm]}\underbrace{\left(\frac{(1-h)}{c}+\frac{1}{c(1+r)}\right)}_{\equiv\theta}\right]$$

which equals (7.3). □

References

Acemoglu, D., Angrist, J., 2000. How large are human-capital externalities? Evidence from compulsory schooling laws. NBER Macroeconomics Annual 15, 9–59.

Angrist, J. D., Krueger, A. B., 1991. Does compulsory school attendance affect schooling and earnings? Quartely Journal of Economics 106, 979–1014.

Arrow, K., 1993. Excellence and equity in higher education. Education Economics 1, 5–12.

Atkinson, A. B., Stiglitz, J. E., 1985. Lectures on Public Economics. McGraw-Hill, New York.

Baran, P. A., Sweezy, P. M., 1966. Monopoly Capital. An Essay on the American Economic and Social Order. Monthly Review Press, New York.

Barbaro, S., 2001. Profitieren die *Reichen* auf Kosten der *Armen* von der öffentlichen Hochschulfinanzierung? Tragen Akademiker die Kosten ihres Studiums? Einige methodologische Anmerkungen zum Forschungsstand über die Verteilungswirkungen der öffentlichen Hochschulfinanzierung in der BRD. Hochschule Ost 10, 254–289.

Barbaro, S., 2003a. The distributional impact of subsidies to higher education - Emprical evidence from Germany. Finanzarchiv N.F. 59, 458–478.

Barbaro, S., 2003b. Neuere Entwicklungen in der Bildungsökonomie. List-Forum für Wirtschafts- und Finanzpolitik 29 (3), 237–248.

Barbaro, S., Südekum, J., 2005a. The interaction of tax exemptions and individual tax reform preferences. iza Discussion Paper Series 1543.

Barbaro, S., Südekum, J., 2005b. Reforming a complicated income-tax system: The political economics perspective. European Journal of Political Economy 22, (forthcoming).

Barbaro, S., Wohlfahrt, G., March, 30 1999. Der Mythos von der Umverteilung. Frankfurter Rundschau (76).

Bareis, P., Erhardt, M., Grüske, K.-D., Klemm, K., Lüthje, J., Müller-Böling, D., Sandberger, G., Ziegele, F., 1999. InvestiF und GefoS. Modelle der individuellen und institutionellen Bildungsfinanzierung im Hochschulbereich. CHE, Guetersloh.

Barr, N., 1989. Student Loans: The Next Steps. University Press, Aberdeen.

Barr, N., 1993. Alternative funding rescources for higher education. The Economic Journal 103, 718–728.

Beckmann, K., 2003. Wer bezahlt die (Hochschul)-Bildung? In: Fraktion Die Grünen/ Bündnis90 im Bundestag (Ed.), Wege aus der Bildungsmisere: Impulse für mehr Gerechtigkeit und Qualität. BT-Fraktion B90/Die Grünen, Berlin, pp. 35–47.

Bedau, K.-D., Teichmann, D., 1995. Die Belastung der privaten Haushalte in West- und Ostdeutschland durch direkte und indirekte Steuern. DIW-Wochenberichte 62, 781–788.

Benabou, R., 2000. Unequal societies: Income distribution and the social contract. American Economic Review 90, 96–129.

Benabou, R., 2002. Tax and education policy in a heterogeneous agent economy: What levels of redistribution maximize growth and efficiency? Econometrica 70, 481–517.

Biewen, M., 2002. Bootstrap inference for inequality, mobility and poverty measurement. Journal of Econometrics 108, 317–342.

Bils, M., Klenow, P. J., 2000. Does schooling cause growth? American Economic Review 90, 1160–1183.

Blaug, M., 1970. An Introduction to the Economics of Education. Penguin, London.

Blaug, M., 1980. Student loans and the NUS. Economic Affairs 1, 45–56.

Blaug, M., 1982. The distributional effects of higher education subsidies. Economics of Education Review 2, 209–231.

Blossfeld, H.-P., Shavit, Y., 1993. Persistent Inequality. Changing Educational Attainment in Thirteen Countries. Westview Press, Oxford.

bmbf, 1999a. Grund- und Strukturdaten. bmbf, Bonn.

bmbf, 1999b. Student Life in Germany. The Socio-Economic Picture. Summary of the 15th Social Survey of the Deutsches Studentenwerk (DSW). bmbf, Bonn.

bmbf, 2002. Grund- und Strukturdaten. bmbf, Bonn.

Bovenberg, A. L., Jacobs, B., 2005. Redistribution and education subsidies are Siamese twins. Journal of Public Economics 90, (forthcoming).

Bowman, M. J., Millot, B., Schiefelbein, E., 1986. An adult life cycle perspective on public subsidies to higher education in three countries. Economics of Education Review 5, 135–145.

Buhmann, B., Rainwater, L., Schmaus, G., Smeeding, T., 1988. Equivalence scales, well-being, inequality, and poverty: sensitivity estimates across ten countries using the Luxembourg Income Study (LIS) database. Review of Income and Wealth 34, 115–142.

Burr, D., 1994. A comparision of certain bootstrap confidence intervals in the Cox model. Journal of the American Statistical Association 89, 1290–1296.

Cameron, S. V., Heckman, J. J., 2001. The dynamics of educational attainment for Black, Hispanic, and White males. Journal of Political Economy 109, 455–499.

Carneiro, P., Heckman, J. J., 2002. The evidence on credit constraints in post-secondary schooling. The Economics Journal 112, 705–734.
Centrum für Hochschulentwicklung, 2003. Akzeptanz von Studiengebühren. CHE, Gütersloh.
Cohn, E., Gifford, A., Sharkansyk, I., 1970. Benefits and costs of higher education and income redistribution: Three comments. Journal of Human Resources 5, 222–236.
Conlisk, J., 1977. A further look at the Hansen-Weisbrod-Pechman debate. Journal of Human Resources 12, 147–163.
Crean, J. F., 1975. The income redistributive effects of public spending on higher education. Journal of Human Resources 10, 116–123.
Creedy, J., François, P., 1990. Financing higher education and majority voting. Journal of Public Economics 43, 181–200.
Dalgaard, P., 2002. Introductory Statistics with R. Statistics and Computing. Springer, New York.
Davidson, C., Segerstrom, P., 1998. R&D subsidies and economic grwoth. RAND Journal of Economics 29 (3), 548–577.
Davison, A. C., Hinkley, D. V., 1997. Bootstrap Methods and their Applications. Cambridge University Press.
DiCiccio, T. J., Efron, B., 1996. Bootstrap confidence intervals. Statistical Science 11 (3), 189–212.
Dupor, B., Lochner, L., Taber, C., Wittekind, M., 1998. Some effects of taxes on schooling and training. American Economic Review—PaP 88, 340–346.
Dur, R. A. J., Teulings, C. N., 2003. Education and efficient redistribution. Tinbergen Institute Discussion Paper TI 2001-090/3 .
Dur, R. A. J., Teulings, C. N., 2004. Are education subsidies an efficient redistributive device? In: Agell, J., Keene, M., Weichenrieder, A. (Eds.), Labor Market Institutions and Public Regulation. MIT-Press, Boston, pp. 123–162.
Eaton, J., Rosen, H. S., 1980. Taxation, human capital, and uncertainty. American Economic Review 70 (4), 705–715.
Efron, B., Tibshirani, R. J., 1986. Bootstrap methods for standard errors, confidence intervals, and other measures of statistical accuracy. Statistical Science 1 (1), 54–77.
Efron, B., Tibshirani, R. J., 1993. An Introduction to the Bootstrap. Chapman and Hall, New York.
Epple, D., Romano, R. E., 1998. Competition between private and public schools, vouchers, and peer-group effects. American Economic Review 88, 33–62.
Faik, J., 1998. Institutionelle Äquivalenzskalen als Basis von Verteilungsanalysen - Eine Modifizierung der Sozialhilfe-Skala. In: Becker, I., Hauser, R. (Eds.), Einkommensverteilung und Armut. Deutschland auf dem Weg in die Vierfünftel-Gesellschaft? Campus, pp. 13–42.
Fernandez, R., Rogerson, R., 1995. On the political economy of education subsidies. Review of Economic Studies 62, 249–262.

Fields, G. S., 1975. Higher education and income distribution in a less developed country. Oxford Economic Papers 27, 245–259.

Friedman, M., 1962. Capitalism and Freedom. The University of Chicago Press, Chicago.

Friedman, M., Friedman, R., 1979. Free to Choose. A Personal Statement. Harcourt Brace Jovanovich, New York and London.

García-Peñalosa, C., Wälde, K., 2000. Efficiency and equity effects of subsidies to higher education. Oxford Economic Papers 52, 702–722.

Glennerster, H., 2003. A graduate tax revisited. Higher Education Review 35, 25–26.

Glennerster, H., Merrett, S., Wilson, G., 2003. A graduate tax. Higher Education Review 35, 27–37.

Greenaway, D., Haynes, M., 2003. Funding higher education in the UK: The role of fees and loans. Economic Journal 113, F150–F166.

Grüske, K.-D., 1978. Die personale Budgetinzidenz. Eine Analyse für die Bundesrepublik. Vandenhoeck and Ruprecht, Göttingen.

Grüske, K.-D., 1994. Verteilungseffekte der öffentlichen Hochschulfinanzierung in der Bundesrepublik Deutschland - Personale Inzidenz im Querschnitt und Längsschnitt. In: Luedecke, R. (Ed.), Bildung, Bildungsfinanzierung und Einkommensverteilung. Vol. 2. Springer, pp. 71–147.

Haisken-DeNew, J., Frick, J., 2000. DTC - Desktop Companion to the German Socio-Economic Panel (GSOEP) Study. DIW, Berlin.

Hall, P., 1992. The Bootstrap and Edgeworth Expansion. Springer, Berlin.

Hansen, L. W., Weisbrod, B. A., 1969a. Benefits, Costs, and Finance of Public Higher Education. Markham, Chicago.

Hansen, L. W., Weisbrod, B. A., 1969b. The distribution of costs and direct benefits of public higher education: The case of California. Journal of Human Resources 4, 176–191.

Hansen, L. W., Weisbrod, B. A., 1971. On the distribution of costs of public higher education: Reply. Journal of Human Resources 6, 363–374.

Hansen, L. W., Weisbrod, B. A., 1978. The distribution of subsidies to students in California public higher education: Reply. Journal of Human Resources 13, 137–139.

Harms, P., Zink, S., 2003. Limits to redistribution in a democracy: A survey. European Journal of Political Economy 19, 651–668.

Hartmann, R. W., 1970. A comment on the Pechman-Hansen-Weisbrod controversy. Journal of Human Resources 5, 519–523.

Haveman, R. H., 1988. Starting Even. An equal opportunity program to combat the Nation's new poverty. Simon and Schuster, New York.

Haveman, R. H., Wolfe, B. L., 1984. Schooling and economic well-being: The role of nonmarket effects. Journal of Human Resources 14, 377–407.

Heckman, J. J., 1976. A life-cycle model of earnings, learning, and consumption. Journal of Political Economy 84, S11–S84.

Helberger, C., 1982. Auswirkungen öffentlicher Bildungsausgaben in der Bundesrepublik Deutschland auf die Einkommensverteilung der Ausbildungsgeneration. Vol. 4 of Schriften des Berichts der Transfer-Enquête-Kommission *Das Transfersystem in der Bundesrepublik Deutschland.* Kohlhammer.

James, E., Benjamin, G., 1987. Educational distribution and income redistribution through education in Japan. Journal of Human Resources 22, 469–489.

Johnson, G. E., 1984. Subsidies for higher education. Journal of Labour Economics 2, 303–318.

Keane, M. P., Wolpin, K. I., 2001. The effect of parental transfers and borrowing constraints on educational attainment. International Economic Review 42, 1051–1103.

Krämer, W., 1999. Falscher Ruf nach Gerechtigkeit. Forschung & Lehre , 401–404.

Krueger, A. B., Lindahl, M., 2001. Education for growth: Why and for whom? Journal of Economic Literature 39, 1101–1136.

Lemelin, C., 1992. Short-term redistributive effects of public financing of university education in Quebec. Canadian Public Policy—Analyse de Politiques 18, 176–188.

Levhari, D., Weiss, Y., 1974. The effect of risk on the investment in human capital. American Economic Review 64, 950–963.

Lincoln, I., Walker, A., 1993. Increasing investment in higher education: The role of a graduate tax. Education Economics 1, 211–226.

Mac Kinnon, J., 2002. Bootstrap inference in econometrics. Canadian Journal of Economics 35, 615–645.

Machlis, P. D., 1973. The distributional effects of public higher education in New York City. Public Finance Quarterly 1, 35–75.

Mare, R. D., 1980. Social background and school continuation decisions. Journal of the American Statistical Association 75, 295–305.

Mare, R. D., 1993. Educational stratification on observed and unobserved components of familiy background. In: Blossfeld, H.-P., Shavit, Y. (Eds.), Persistent Inequality. Changing Educational Attainment in Thirteen Countries. Westview Press, pp. 351–376.

Marx, K., Engels, F., 1875[1962]. Kritik des Gothaer Programms. Dietz, Berlin.

McGuire, J. W., 1976. The distribution of subsidies to students in California public higher education. Journal of Human Resources 11, 343–353.

McPherson, M. S., Shapiro, M. O., 1991. Does students aid affect college enrollment? New evidence on a persistent controversy. American Economic Review 81, 309–318.

Merz, D., 1981. Umverteilungswirkungen der schweizerischen Hochschulpolitik. Dietz, Basel.

Mill, J. S., 1848[1994]. Principles of Political Economy. Oxford University Press, Oxford.

Mills, J. A., Zandvakili, S., 1997. Statistical inference via bootstrapping for measures of inequality. Journal of Applied Econometrics 12, 133–150.

Mincer, J., 1958. Investment in human capital and personal income distribution. Journal of Political Economy 66, 281–302.

Mirrless, J. A., 1971. An exploration in the theory of optimum income taxation. Review of Economic Studies 38, 175–208.

Musgrave, R. A., Musgrave, P. B., 1984. Public Finance in Theory and Practice. McGraw Hill, New York.

Musgrave, R. A., Thin, T., 1948. Income tax progression, 1929 - 1948. Journal of Political Economy 56, 498–514.

Norregaard, J., 1990. Progressivity of income tax systems. OECD Economic Studies 15, 83–110.

OECD, 1993. Education at a Glance. OECD Indicators 1993. OECD, Paris.

OECD, 2002. Education at a Glance. OECD Indicators 2002. OECD, Paris.

Pechman, J. A., 1970. The distributional effects of public higher education in California. Journal of Human Resources 5, 361–370.

Pechman, J. A., 1972. Note on the intergenerational transfer of public higher-education benefits. Journal of Political Economy 80, S256–S259.

Pechman, J. A., 1986. The Rich, the Poor, and the Taxes they Pay. Wheatsheaf Books, Sussex.

Pennings, E., 2000. Taxes and stimuli of investment under uncertainty. European Economic Review 44, 383–391.

Perotti, R., 1993. Political equilibrium, income distribution, and growth. Review of Economic Studies 60, 755–776.

Picht, G., 1964. Die deutsche Bildungskatastrophe. Walter, Olten.

Pollak, H., 1980. Steuertarife. In: Neumark, F. (Ed.), Handbuch der Finanzwissenschaft. Vol. 2. Mohr, Tübingen, pp. 239–266.

Poutvaara, P., 2004. Educating Europe: Should public education be financed with graduate taxes or income-contingent loans? CESifo Economic Studies 50, 663–684.

Poutvaara, P., Kanniainen, V., 2000. Why invest in your neighbor? Social contract on educational investment. International Tax and Public Finance 7, 574–562.

R Development Core Team, 2004. R: A language and environment for statistical computing. R Foundation for Statistical Computing, Vienna, Austria, ISBN 3-900051-07-0.
URL `http://www.R-project.org`

Richter, W., 1999. Entstaatlichungspotentiale im Hochschulbereich. Gutachten für den Sachverständigenrat zur Begutachtung der gesamtwirtschaftlichen Entwicklung. In: Helmstädter, E. (Ed.), Vorträge. No. 442 in Nordrhein-Westfälische Akademie der Wissenschaften. Westdeutscher Verlag, pp. 37–68.

Sachverständigenrat Bildung, 1998. Für ein verändertes System der Bildungsfinanzierung. Hans-Böckler-Stiftung.

Saint-Paul, G., Verdier, T., 1993. Education, democracy and growth. Journal of Development Economics , 399–407.

Sen, A., 1997. On Economic Inequality. Clarendon Press, Oxford.

Shea, J., 2000. Does parent's money matter? Journal of Public Economics 77, 155–184.
Sheshinski, E., 1972. The optimal linear income tax. Review of Economic Studies 39, 297–302.
Shorrocks, A. F., 1982. Inequality decomposition by factor components. Econometrica 50, 193–211.
Sinn, H.-W., 1995. A theory of the welfare state. Scandinavian Journal of Economics 97, 495–526.
Sturn, R., Wohlfahrt, G., 1999. Der gebührenfreie Hochschulzugang und seine Alternativen. Verlag Österreich, Vienna.
Sturn, R., Wohlfahrt, G., 2000. Who pays for higher education? A note on the neglected role of income tax progression. Finanzarchiv N.F. 57, 126–136.
Trostel, P. A., 1993. The effect of taxation on human capital. Journal of Political Economy 101, 327–351.
Trostel, P. A., 1996. Should education be subsidized? Public Finance Quarterly 24, 3–24.
Tsakloglou, P., Antoninis, M., 1999. On the distributional impact of public education: Evidence from Greece. Economics of Education Review 18, 439–452.
Venables, W. N., Smith, D. M., the R Devolopment Core Team, 2001. An Introduction to R. Network Theory, Bristol.
Wigger, B. U., 2004. Are higher education subsidies second best? Scandinavian Journal of Economics 106, 65–82.
Wissenschaftsrat, 1997. Finanzstatistische Kennzahlen ausgewählter Studiengänge. Wissenschaftsrat, Cologne.
Xu, K., 2000. Inference for generalized Gini indices using the iterated-bootstrap method. Journal of Business and Economic Statistics 18, 223–227.
Ziegele, F., Erhardt, M., Müller-Böling, D., 1998. Modell für einen Beitrag der Studierenden zur Finanzierung der Hochschulen (Studienbeitragsmodell). CHE, Guetersloh.

List of Figures

List of Tables

Index

Lecture Notes in Economics and Mathematical Systems

For information about Vols. 1–464
please contact your bookseller or Springer-Verlag

Vol. 465: T. J. Stewart, R. C. van den Honert (Eds.), Trends in Multicriteria Decision Making. X, 448 pages. 1998.

Vol. 466: A. Sadrieh, The Alternating Double Auction Market. VII, 350 pages. 1998.

Vol. 467: H. Hennig-Schmidt, Bargaining in a Video Experiment. Determinants of Boundedly Rational Behavior. XII, 221 pages. 1999.

Vol. 468: A. Ziegler, A Game Theory Analysis of Options. XIV, 145 pages. 1999.

Vol. 469: M. P. Vogel, Environmental Kuznets Curves. XIII, 197 pages. 1999.

Vol. 470: M. Ammann, Pricing Derivative Credit Risk. XII, 228 pages. 1999.

Vol. 471: N. H. M. Wilson (Ed.), Computer-Aided Transit Scheduling. XI, 444 pages. 1999.

Vol. 472: J.-R. Tyran, Money Illusion and Strategic Complementarity as Causes of Monetary Non-Neutrality. X, 228 pages. 1999.

Vol. 473: S. Helber, Performance Analysis of Flow Lines with Non-Linear Flow of Material. IX, 280 pages. 1999.

Vol. 474: U. Schwalbe, The Core of Economies with Asymmetric Information. IX, 141 pages. 1999.

Vol. 475: L. Kaas, Dynamic Macroeconomics with Imperfect Competition. XI, 155 pages. 1999.

Vol. 476: R. Demel, Fiscal Policy, Public Debt and the Term Structure of Interest Rates. X, 279 pages. 1999.

Vol. 477: M. Théra, R. Tichatschke (Eds.), Ill-posed Variational Problems and Regularization Techniques. VIII, 274 pages. 1999.

Vol. 478: S. Hartmann, Project Scheduling under Limited Resources. XII, 221 pages. 1999.

Vol. 479: L. v. Thadden, Money, Inflation, and Capital Formation. IX, 192 pages. 1999.

Vol. 480: M. Grazia Speranza, P. Stähly (Eds.), New Trends in Distribution Logistics. X, 336 pages. 1999.

Vol. 481: V. H. Nguyen, J. J. Strodiot, P. Tossings (Eds.). Optimation. IX, 498 pages. 2000.

Vol. 482: W. B. Zhang, A Theory of International Trade. XI, 192 pages. 2000.

Vol. 483: M. Königstein, Equity, Efficiency and Evolutionary Stability in Bargaining Games with Joint Production. XII, 197 pages. 2000.

Vol. 484: D. D. Gatti, M. Gallegati, A. Kirman, Interaction and Market Structure. VI, 298 pages. 2000.

Vol. 485: A. Garnaev, Search Games and Other Applications of Game Theory. VIII, 145 pages. 2000.

Vol. 486: M. Neugart, Nonlinear Labor Market Dynamics. X, 175 pages. 2000.

Vol. 487: Y. Y. Haimes, R. E. Steuer (Eds.), Research and Practice in Multiple Criteria Decision Making. XVII, 553 pages. 2000.

Vol. 488: B. Schmolck, Ommitted Variable Tests and Dynamic Specification. X, 144 pages. 2000.

Vol. 489: T. Steger, Transitional Dynamics and Economic Growth in Developing Countries. VIII, 151 pages. 2000.

Vol. 490: S. Minner, Strategic Safety Stocks in Supply Chains. XI, 214 pages. 2000.

Vol. 491: M. Ehrgott, Multicriteria Optimization. VIII, 242 pages. 2000.

Vol. 492: T. Phan Huy, Constraint Propagation in Flexible Manufacturing. IX, 258 pages. 2000.

Vol. 493: J. Zhu, Modular Pricing of Options. X, 170 pages. 2000.

Vol. 494: D. Franzen, Design of Master Agreements for OTC Derivatives. VIII, 175 pages. 2001.

Vol. 495: I. Konnov, Combined Relaxation Methods for Variational Inequalities. XI, 181 pages. 2001.

Vol. 496: P. Weiß, Unemployment in Open Economies. XII, 226 pages. 2001.

Vol. 497: J. Inkmann, Conditional Moment Estimation of Nonlinear Equation Systems. VIII, 214 pages. 2001.

Vol. 498: M. Reutter, A Macroeconomic Model of West German Unemployment. X, 125 pages. 2001.

Vol. 499: A. Casajus, Focal Points in Framed Games. XI, 131 pages. 2001.

Vol. 500: F. Nardini, Technical Progress and Economic Growth. XVII, 191 pages. 2001.

Vol. 501: M. Fleischmann, Quantitative Models for Reverse Logistics. XI, 181 pages. 2001.

Vol. 502: N. Hadjisavvas, J. E. Martínez-Legaz, J.-P. Penot (Eds.), Generalized Convexity and Generalized Monotonicity. IX, 410 pages. 2001.

Vol. 503: A. Kirman, J.-B. Zimmermann (Eds.), Economics with Heterogenous Interacting Agents. VII, 343 pages. 2001.

Vol. 504: P.-Y. Moix (Ed.),The Measurement of Market Risk. XI, 272 pages. 2001.

Vol. 505: S. Voß, J. R. Daduna (Eds.), Computer-Aided Scheduling of Public Transport. XI, 466 pages. 2001.

Vol. 506: B. P. Kellerhals, Financial Pricing Models in Con-tinuous Time and Kalman Filtering. XIV, 247 pages. 2001.

Vol. 507: M. Koksalan, S. Zionts, Multiple Criteria Decision Making in the New Millenium. XII, 481 pages. 2001.

Vol. 508: K. Neumann, C. Schwindt, J. Zimmermann, Project Scheduling with Time Windows and Scarce Resources. XI, 335 pages. 2002.

Vol. 509: D. Hornung, Investment, R&D, and Long-Run Growth. XVI, 194 pages. 2002.

Vol. 510: A. S. Tangian, Constructing and Applying Objective Functions. XII, 582 pages. 2002.

Vol. 511: M. Külpmann, Stock Market Overreaction and Fundamental Valuation. IX, 198 pages. 2002.

Vol. 512: W.-B. Zhang, An Economic Theory of Cities.XI, 220 pages. 2002.

Vol. 513: K. Marti, Stochastic Optimization Techniques. VIII, 364 pages. 2002.

Vol. 514: S. Wang, Y. Xia, Portfolio and Asset Pricing. XII, 200 pages. 2002.

Vol. 515: G. Heisig, Planning Stability in Material Requirements Planning System. XII, 264 pages. 2002.

Vol. 516: B. Schmid, Pricing Credit Linked Financial Instruments. X, 246 pages. 2002.

Vol. 517: H. I. Meinhardt, Cooperative Decision Making in Common Pool Situations. VIII, 205 pages. 2002.

Vol. 518: S. Napel, Bilateral Bargaining. VIII, 188 pages. 2002.

Vol. 519: A. Klose, G. Speranza, L. N. Van Wassenhove (Eds.), Quantitative Approaches to Distribution Logistics and Supply Chain Management. XIII, 421 pages. 2002.

Vol. 520: B. Glaser, Efficiency versus Sustainability in Dynamic Decision Making. IX, 252 pages. 2002.

Vol. 521: R. Cowan, N. Jonard (Eds.), Heterogenous Agents, Interactions and Economic Performance. XIV, 339 pages. 2003.

Vol. 522: C. Neff, Corporate Finance, Innovation, and Strategic Competition. IX, 218 pages. 2003.

Vol. 523: W.-B. Zhang, A Theory of Interregional Dynamics. XI, 231 pages. 2003.

Vol. 524: M. Frölich, Programme Evaluation and Treatment Choise. VIII, 191 pages. 2003.

Vol. 525: S. Spinler, Capacity Reservation for Capital-Intensive Technologies. XVI, 139 pages. 2003.

Vol. 526: C. F. Daganzo, A Theory of Supply Chains. VIII, 123 pages. 2003.

Vol. 527: C. E. Metz, Information Dissemination in Currency Crises. XI, 231 pages. 2003.

Vol. 528: R. Stolletz, Performance Analysis and Optimization of Inbound Call Centers. X, 219 pages. 2003.

Vol. 529: W. Krabs, S. W. Pickl, Analysis, Controllability and Optimization of Time-Discrete Systems and Dynamical Games. XII, 187 pages. 2003.

Vol. 530: R. Wapler, Unemployment, Market Structure and Growth. XXVII, 207 pages. 2003.

Vol. 531: M. Gallegati, A. Kirman, M. Marsili (Eds.), The Complex Dynamics of Economic Interaction. XV, 402 pages, 2004.

Vol. 532: K. Marti, Y. Ermoliev, G. Pflug (Eds.), Dynamic Stochastic Optimization. VIII, 336 pages. 2004.

Vol. 533: G. Dudek, Collaborative Planning in Supply Chains. X, 234 pages. 2004.

Vol. 534: M. Runkel, Environmental and Resource Policy for Consumer Durables. X, 197 pages. 2004.

Vol. 535: X. Gandibleux, M. Sevaux, K. Sörensen, V.T'kindt (Eds.), Metaheuristics for Multiobjective Optimisation. IX, 249 pages. 2004.

Vol. 536: R. Brüggemann, Model Reduction Methods for Vector Autoregressive Processes. X, 218 pages. 2004.

Vol. 537: A. Esser, Pricing in (In)Complete Markets. XI, 122 pages, 2004.

Vol. 538: S. Kokot, The Econometrics of Sequential Trade Models. XI, 193 pages. 2004.

Vol. 539: N. Hautsch, Modelling Irregularly Spaced Financial Data. XII, 291 pages. 2004.

Vol. 540: H. Kraft, Optimal Portfolios with Stochastic Interest Rates and Defaultable Assets. X, 173 pages. 2004.

Vol. 541: G.-y. Chen, X. Huang, X. Yang, Vector Optimization. X, 306 pages. 2005.

Vol. 542: J. Lingens, Union Wage Bargaining and Economic Growth. XIII, 199 pages. 2004.

Vol. 543: C. Benkert, Default Risk in Bond and Credit Derivatives Markets. IX, 135 pages. 2004.

Vol. 544: B. Fleischmann, A. Klose, Distribution Logistics. X, 284 pages. 2004.

Vol. 545: R. Hafner, Stochastic Implied Volatility. XI, 229 pages. 2004.

Vol. 546: D. Quadt, Lot-Sizing and Scheduling for Flexible Flow Lines. XVIII, 227 pages. 2004.

Vol. 547: M. Wildi, Signal Extraction. XI, 279 pages. 2005.

Vol. 548: D. Kuhn, Generalized Bounds for Convex Multistage Stochastic Programs. XI, 190 pages. 2005.

Vol. 549: G. N. Krieg, Kanban-Controlled Manufacturing Systems. IX, 236 pages. 2005.

Vol. 550: T. Lux, S. Reitz, E. Samanidou, Nonlinear Dynamics and Heterogeneous Interacting Agents. XIII, 327 pages. 2005.

Vol. 551: J. Leskow, M. Puchet Anyul, L. F. Punzo, New Tools of Economic Dynamics. XIX, 392 pages. 2005.

Vol. 552: C. Suerie, Time Continuity in Discrete Time Models. XVIII, 229 pages. 2005.

Vol. 553: B. Mönch, Strategic Trading in Illiquid Markets. XIII, 116 pages. 2005.

Vol. 554: R. Foellmi, Consumption Structure and Macroeconomics. IX, 152 pages. 2005.

Vol. 555: J. Wenzelburger, Learning in Economic Systems with Expectations Feedback (planned) 2005.

Vol. 556: R. Branzei, D. Dimitrov, S. Tijs, Models in Cooperative Game Theory. VIII, 135 pages. 2005.

Vol. 557: S. Barbaro, Equity and Efficiency Considerations of Public Higer Education. XII, 128 pages. 2005.

Vol. 558: M. Faliva, Topics in Dynamic Model Analysis. X, 144 pages. 2005.

Vol. 559: M. Schulmerich, Real Options Valuation. XVI, 357 pages. 2005.